INVISIBLE WORK, INVISIBLE WORKERS

Also by Madeleine Leonard

INFORMAL ECONOMIC ACTIVITY IN BELFAST

WOMEN AND IRISH SOCIETY: A Sociological Reader (*co-editor with Anne Byrne*)

Invisible Work, Invisible Workers

The Informal Economy in Europe and the US

Madeleine Leonard
Department of Sociology and Social Policy
Queen's University
Belfast

First published in Great Britain 1998 by
MACMILLAN PRESS LTD
Houndmills, Basingstoke, Hampshire RG21 6XS and London
Companies and representatives throughout the world

A catalogue record for this book is available from the British Library.

ISBN 0–333–63797–6

First published in the United States of America 1998 by
ST. MARTIN'S PRESS, INC.,
Scholarly and Reference Division,
175 Fifth Avenue, New York, N.Y. 10010

ISBN 0–312–21760–9

Library of Congress Cataloging-in-Publication Data
Leonard, Madeleine.
Invisible work, invisible workers : the informal economy in Europe
and the US / Madeleine Leonard.
p. cm.
Includes bibliographical references and index.
ISBN 0–312–21760–9 (cloth)
1. Informal sector (Economics)—Europe. 2. Informal sector
(Economics)—United States. I. Title.
HD2346.E9L46   1998
381—dc21
                                              98–23857
                                                CIP

This book is printed on paper suitable for recycling and made from fully managed and
sustained forest sources.

10   9   8   7   6   5   4   3   2   1
07   06   05   04   03   02   01   00   99   98

Printed and bound in Great Britain by
Antony Rowe Ltd, Chippenham, Wiltshire

Contents

Dedicated to the memory of Gareth (Dubbs) Wilson

1 Introduction

Of all the transformations that have characterized the 20th century, one of the most significant has been in the sphere of work. While the beginning of the 20th century witnessed widespread, rapid growth in formal employment, the end of the 20th century has been marked by the emergence of new forms of work, rising unemployment and the persistence and resilience of informal economic activity. Initially viewed as a remnant of traditionalism and associated with cities in developing societies, the informal economy has emerged as a central feature of economic development. No matter what kind of society one looks at, be it advanced capitalist, socialist or post-communist, informal economic activity contributes significantly to the overall economy. This book is concerned with examining the nature, extent, and significance of the informal economy in the United States and Western European countries. This topic is highly complex because of the varied meanings attached to the phenomenon, difficulties in ascertaining its size and because of the complex differences within and between countries exhibiting informal economic practices. Such an analysis prompts consideration of the role of the state in shaping the structure of national economies. As states have adopted regulative systems for wage rates, health and safety requirements, collecting taxes and establishing welfare systems, they have encouraged the development of irregular employment strategies. Avoiding over burdensome state regulation provides an incentive for tax evasion, welfare benefit abuse and a multitude of other activities aimed at earning invisible income. The state has also supported capitalism's increasing emphasis on flexibility by easing the way for the introduction of non-standard forms of employment. The analysis does not end here as an exclusive focus on market activity ignores a host of activities that take place outside the formal market place. These activities are embedded in households and communities and throw up all sorts of questions concerning the distinction between work and employment in advanced capitalist societies.

DEFINING THE INFORMAL ECONOMY

Defining the informal economy is no easy task. No one all-embracing definition exists. Rather a multitude of terms, practices and definitions abound and these are exacerbated by regional and national differences over regulation, so that an activity might be an acceptable regular feature of the economy in one country yet consigned to the informal sector in another. These issues will be explored in Chapter 2. As a working definition, I use the term to describe economic activity which is not recorded in official statistics and which operates in the absence of administrative monitoring and control. While this interpretation accords with the standard definition of the informal economy in social science literature in that it excludes criminal activities, the analysis here goes beyond definitions which are limited to the illegal pursuit of legal economic ends (DeSoto, 1989). Focusing on state regulation of labour market activities ignores the myriad of ways in which economic behaviour is embedded in social relations within households and communities where exchanges of goods and services often take place outside market forces. While these activities are less interesting to those concerned with state regulation and fiscal affairs, nonetheless, they are fundamental to understanding the complexity of economic life as individuals, households and communities strive to achieve a modicum of security in an otherwise unstable, formal economic environment.

Concentrating on state regulation introduces one of the key arguments of the book and that is that it is impossible to define the informal economy without firstly defining the formal economy. This approach views the informal economy as inextricably related to the formal economy and challenges notions of separateness that have appeared in some definitions (Shankland, 1984). It also implies that definition has as much to do with state regulation as the economic and social relations under which such activities are carried out. Indeed, it is the increasing bureaucratization of the state that leads to the emergence of activities which fall outside its realm of monitoring and control. Much of the official interest in the informal economy has been concerned with estimating its size for the purposes of accurately calculating GNP and the level of tax governments should obtain from their citizens. Interest has also been spurned by the need to cut back on welfare systems and hence incidents of potential welfare abuse are avidly seized upon by those concerned with limiting state spending in this area. Hence, state regulation of economic activity is a major device used to differentiate between formal, regular, legal economic activity and informal, irregular and illegal economic activity.

DIFFERENTIATING BETWEEN WORK AND EMPLOYMENT

The separation between work and employment is one of the key themes of the book. Much of the literature on the informal economy is fraught with terminological confusion particularly its tendency to collapse the categories of work and employment under the umbrella term of work (Harding and Jenkins, 1989). The development of capitalist social and economic relations led to the development of complex distinctions between work and employment. The increasing bureaucratization of economic activity introduced a gradual separation of work from employment. Individuals became categorized as employed, self-employed or unemployed depending on their formal participation in labour market activity. To be classified as 'working' or being 'economically active' meant engaging in some form of employment in the formal labour market. Activities which fell outside the realm of formal employment were dismissed as non-work or non-economic. From the 1970s onwards, there was an increasing recognition that individuals might be brought into the formal labour market in informal ways. The term 'informal work' was used to classify the diverse range of practices whereby individuals might be economically active outside formal employment. However, this catch-all phrase blurred the differences between activities characterized by an employment relationship, albeit an informal one, and activities where such a relationship was absent. Some activities are primarily market orientated and involve working for an employer or working for a customer, while other activities are qualitatively different from the employment relationship. These latter activities are embedded in complex social relationships and take place within households and communities. Payment may be in cash and kind and while the profit motive may be present in some of these exchanges, others are characterized by norms of reciprocity. These distinctions are reflected in the range of economic activities covered in the book.

Chapter 3 focuses on the various non-standard and increasingly flexible forms of employment generated by the current restructuring of capitalism. The chapter draws on recent perspectives on the informal economy which emphasize the efforts of industry to decentralize and reduce costs in the face of heightened international competition. One integral element of the strategies of capitalist accumulation adopted by modern firms, particularly small-scale, concerns bypassing, where possible, state and union control. Firms can achieve this in one of two main ways, either hiring labour off-the-books or subcontracting production and services out to smaller, less regulated enterprises. Hence state regulation provides a key incentive for firms to engage in casual hiring and informal subcontracting (Portes and Schauffler, 1992). Instead of core and periphery workers, there are now core and periphery firms. Large scale firms spin off into medium-size, medium-skilled firms which then spin off their own less skilled production units on to subcontractors (Lash, 1994). Escaping the regulatory operations of the formal economy enhances the economic opportunities of such firms and paves the way for the development of informal employment opportunities.

Of course, one might argue that there is nothing new about exploitative relationships of production. Sweatshops, for example, have always existed. They were a central component in the early phase of capitalist accumulation and their survival tells us little about current processes in advanced capitalism. Recent researchers have, however, challenged this assumption (Sassen, 1991; Castells and Portes, 1989) by arguing that old practices in new contexts are in fact new. The key to understanding the uniqueness of modern day sweatshops is that they function in the midst of institutional regulation. This separates modern day versions of sweatshops from their classic predecessors which operated in largely unregulated environments. This introduces a crucial point and that is that while certain activities may lend themselves to informalization, it is not their inherent qualities but rather the confines of state regulation that determine informalization (Sassen, 1991:80). Since these regulations will differ from one country to another then so will the definition of what is formal and informal. Nonetheless, there are some universal trends in the labour process that encourage informalization and while such trends may have regionally or nationally specific consequences, unravelling the common aspects of such trends may contribute to our overall understanding of the informal economy. Chapter 3 looks at the ways in which these processes operate in different countries and indeed in different regions within the same country. The analysis centres on prominent trends prevalent in the restructuring of the world economy.

INFORMAL EMPLOYMENT: STRATEGIES OF INDIVIDUALS

Chapter 4 concentrates on the individuals and groups affected by these processes by seeking to determine who is employed informally. This is not to suggest that informalization inevitably resides in the characteristics of the workforce but exploring the actual employment and work practices of frequent participants may enhance our understanding of the wider developments which induce such informalization. The chapter includes moonlighters, the unemployed, immigrants, and children who gain access to informal employment. The list is not meant to be an exhaustive account of the various forms of informal employment but rather is a snapshot of the types of work and groups of people which exemplify the increasing trend towards flexibility.

Moonlighting reminds us of the inter-relationship between the formal and informal economy as the same workers may alternate between the two sectors and combine employment in both (Roberts, 1989). In some instances, moonlighting is connected to one's occupation in the formal economy while in other instances individuals may simultaneously engage in a completely different occupation. Some countries, such as Italy, collect statistics on multiple job holders while other countries define workers in terms of their primary occupation thus enhancing the invisibility of moonlighting activities. Earning extra income is the main motivation for becoming involved in moonlighting and this need may be present among professionals as well as the unskilled formally employed population. In some cases, the fall in real wages and status associated with professions such as teaching may necessitate involvement in extra work such as personal tuition to secure an above average life-style. At the lower end of the scale, amalgamating income from a range of low-paid occupations may provide participants with the revenue necessary to maintain an acceptable living standard and participate in increasingly consumer orientated societies. The chapter examines the extent of moonlighting in a range of different countries.

Most studies of the informal economy suggest that the unemployed are the least likely but most widely publicized group commonly assumed to become involved in informal economic activity. Chapter 4 examines the links between unemployment and informal economic activity in a range of different economic settings. Countries with advanced welfare systems which provide economic assistance to the unemployed make it very difficult for welfare recipients to engage in many forms of paid employment. While some countries may have an earnings disregard, this is likely to be so low that it acts as a disincentive to 'working' while claiming welfare assistance since the income earned may have an adverse affect on benefit entitlements. Losing unemployment benefits may act as a major deterrent to individuals selling their labour power informally. Collecting hard data on the involvement of the unemployed in informal employment is fraught with difficulties. The unemployed are unlikely to admit to participation since this particular practice is viewed more negatively than other types of informal employment. In the absence of reliable data, exaggerated estimates often motivated by political concerns rather than objective data surround the whole area. This type of informal employment also has the most policy implications as it provides states with justifications for cutting back on welfare provision. The chapter will outline the tendency for the unemployed when working informally to be involved in aspects of the labour process which are labour intensive, unskilled, low-status and where opportunities for exploitation are very pronounced.

Recent international migration in both Europe and the United States has created an abundant supply of low-wage labour. State migration policies were initially motivated by the needs of industry for unskilled and semi-skilled labour. However, as supply outstripped demand, opportunities for the overflow to obtain irregular informal employment rather than regular formal employment grew. This is not to say that the existence of an informal economy in developed societies is simply due to large numbers of immigrants entering developed countries. As the rest of the chapter points out, children, students, the indigenous unemployed and formally employed all participate to varying degrees in informal economic activity. What needs to be explained here is how large groups of immigrant workers provide willing recruits for the downgraded work opportunities that characterize many growing sectors of the formal economy. Such a perspective will challenge the commonly held view that informalization is simply due to the survival strategies of immigrants and could be retracted by tightening immigration policies. The chapter illustrates how immigrant involvement in the informal economy is linked to the structural requirements of developed societies.

Though reliable statistics are rare, available information suggests that the number of working children remains extremely high in European countries and the United States. The growth of the service sector, the rapid increase in the supply of part-time jobs and the search for a more flexible workforce have contributed to the expansion of the child labour market. The ILO estimates that 142 000 children work in Spain, 114 000 in Italy and 90 000 in Portugal (van Herpen, 1990). Specifying the phenomenon to be studied is not simple and straightforward as the definition of childhood may differ from one country to another. Moreover, the integration of children into economic life may be a regular feature of the economy in some countries and an irregular feature of others. The chapter explores these issues but pays particular attention to the informal ways in which children are incorporated into the formal labour market.

While each of the above groups are discussed separately, none of the categories are mutually exclusive. Immigrants, for example, may form a substantial proportion of the unemployed or alternatively may be more likely to engage in moonlighting. Hence, there are various overlaps between each type of informal employment. However, for ease of explanation, the distinctions rather than the overlaps will be the primary concern of the chapter.

INFORMAL WORK: STRATEGIES OF HOUSEHOLDS AND COMMUNITIES

Chapter 5 moves the focal point away from individuals towards households and communities. Self provisioning within households, subsistence agriculture and reciprocity are the main themes explored in the chapter. These activities are often viewed as a holdover of backward or traditional economic relations. However, the perspective adopted in the chapter is to see such activities as a persistent feature of capitalist economies. Global recession and restructuring have resulted in the retreat of the state from welfare provision in many countries. Budget restrictions on welfare spending in the United States and many European countries have renewed interest in the economic potential of the caring capacities of households and communities. The chapter looks at how households and communities,

in the absence of formal employment opportunities and effective
welfare provision, adapt to precarious economic circumstances. By
exploiting the economic potential of social and kinship networks
and engaging in self-provisioning, households can adjust to changing economic situations and dilute the imperfections of the formal
labour market. While these forms of work were expected to gradually disappear, the chapter demonstrates that they have, on the
contrary, persisted and in some contexts increased in importance.

WOMEN AND THE INFORMAL ECONOMY

Gender is another crucial factor which structures access to informal economic activity. There has been a tendency to consider participants in the informal economy as a relatively homogeneous mass.
The types of informal employment outlined in Chapter 4 and informal work practices described in Chapter 5 reveal a heterogeneous
mass of individuals and enterprises involved in a host of elaborate
and often vague activities. Women are prototypical informal workers since much of their labour takes place outside the realm of
formal employment. Typically, domestic labour, child-rearing, caring and emotional labour have been seen as non-work and as natural
feminine pursuits. These notions of femininity have affected women's
participation in formal and informal wage labour and other forms
of economic activity outside the formal labour market. Chapter 6
examines women's experiences of informal employment. This is not
to deny the significant economic importance of the various activities women engage in in their roles as 'housewives'. These issues
have been dealt with extensively elsewhere. Here, my concern is
with the economic activities that are often assumed to exemplify
the workings of the informal economy and the subsequent neglect
of the possibility that such practices might be gender specific. The
chapter explores the particular ways in which women are incorporated into the public, yet largely invisible, domain of informal
employment.

ALIENATION AND THE INFORMAL ECONOMY

Chapter 7 assesses the degree to which informal economic activity
can be considered to represent progressive change towards some

level of individual or group autonomy. Positive commentators on the informal economy suggest it has the potential to personalize the experience of work and enhance flexibility in work choices. By working informally, individuals can adapt their time more effectively to cater to family and community needs and achieve this in the absence of excessive bureaucratic state control (Cornuel and Duriez, 1985). While many of the work and employment practices illustrated throughout the book would question the capability of the informal economy to meet this ideal, nonetheless, there is some evidence to indicate that informal work and employment have the potential to challenge the seeming inability of individuals, households and communities to respond to wider national and international economic forces.

CONCLUSIONS

Chapter 8 brings together the main themes of the book and reviews the issues covered in each chapter. There are a number of policy issues emerging from the existence of an informal economy and these are briefly outlined. By definition, the informal economy exists only where a formal system operates. Hence, by eliminating regulation, it should be possible to eliminate the informal sector (Mingione, 1994a). This approach has been adopted by some countries through attempts to 'deregulate' economic activity. However, excessive flexibilization of the labour market involves creating new employment conditions which further erode rather than promote the economic security of those workers employed at the blurred interface between the formal and informal economy. Whatever solutions are adapted, individuals, households and communities will continue to be profoundly influenced by global restructuring in ways which fundamentally shape and influence their daily working practices.

While, where appropriate, I draw on my own research into the informal economy in Northern Ireland, the main purpose of the book is to synthesize the findings of a wide range of existing research into the workings of the informal economy in Western Europe and the United States in order to highlight key trends in the present and future significance of informal work and employment. Such an overview challenges a number of studies into the informal economy which suggest that the phenomenon is little more than an exploitative form of peripheral employment for marginalized groups. To do this, I emphasize this aspect of the informal economy at the expense of other features, in order to demonstrate its importance to the development of new forms of advanced capitalism rather than put forward the traditional view of such activities as a remnant of classic capitalism. Part of this analysis involves reiterating and demonstrating the importance of the social embeddedness of economic activity as a continued feature of capitalist society rather than a left over from a previous era. This is why it is necessary to include the responses of households and communities as well as individuals to changes in the formal world of work and employment.

By highlighting common themes in the literature in the informal economy, there is a danger of collapsing complex features of a heterogeneous mass of activities into an over simplistic framework. My intention here is to explore broad commonalties while keeping in mind the diverse variations in the manifestation of informal working arrangements in different localities, regions and nations and among different groups. Among other things, the book stresses the importance of history and locality, structure and agency, for understanding the nature of the informal economy. Rather than dismissing local and regional studies into the informal economy as partial images of specific trends, I utilize this literature to explore the heterogeneous effects of homogenizing processes. Within this literature, a number of universal processes in the nature of advanced capitalism can be discerned but these tend to have differing effects dependent among other things on how rules and regulations are interpreted and enforced across localities, regions and nations; the role of local, regional and national political actors; the extent and nature of welfare state provision in specific countries and the interaction between individuals' motivations and opportunities to work informally. By exploring these themes, the book illustrates the continued ambiguous nature of work and the ever changing boundaries between formal and informal economic activity.

2 Estimates and Guesstimates: Defining the Informal Economy in Europe and the United States

Defining the informal economy is far from straightforward. The extremely variable fiscal systems and social and cultural structures which characterize countries within Europe and states within America make it impossible to provide an overall definition. The term was first introduced in the context of economic activity in developing societies (Hart, 1973). The phrase was used thereafter as an umbrella term to describe ways of making a living outside the formal wage economy either as an alternative to it or as a means of supplementing income within it (Bromley and Gerry, 1979). In addition to the term, informal economy, Henry (1982:461) suggests that there are at least 15 other labels attached to informal economic activities. These include hidden, black, cash, underground, secondary, domestic, household, criminal and alternative economy.

This confusion over terminology is matched by confusion over what constitutes informal economic activity. Terms such as criminal, domestic and household economy obviously relate to a specific set of activities but it is more difficult to assess what is included in definitions such as underground, secondary and alternative economy. Some researchers have used these definitions to include criminal activity while others have excluded criminal activity focusing on legal activities that escape regulation. Similarly some researchers concentrate on paid informal economic activity and hence exclude unpaid work in the household or community from their analyses. Others incorporate elaborate discussions on the conditions whereby leisure activities, when they are concerned with producing something of material value, are not really leisure activities at all but disguised work.

A range of studies into the supposed existence of an informal economy reflect this confusion. To Feige (1977), the informal economy describes all unreported and unmeasured economic activity falling outside the scope of a nation's techniques for monitoring the economy. For Portes (1981), the informal economy refers to all income-producing activities outside formal sector wages and social security. To Tanzi (1982), the informal economy is gross national product that because of non-reporting and/or under-reporting is not measured by official statistics. Others (Mattera, 1985; Smith, 1986) make distinctions between activities that are merely unmeasured and those that are concealed in order to evade taxation and other regulations while Henry and Mars (1978) distinguish between activities that merely escape regulation and others that are more overtly illegal such as drug trafficking. Hence some activities are informal because there do not exist rules that would formalize them while other activities are informal precisely because there are rules which would regulate them or prohibit the activities involved (Boer, 1990).

The distinctions outlined by the International Labour Office (ILO) typified the research into the informal economy during the late 1960s and early 1970s. The formal economy was characterized by corporate ownership, large-scale operation, difficult entry, capital intensive production, frequent reliance on overseas resources, formally acquired skills and protected markets. The informal economy was considered in terms of opposing characteristics such as family ownership, small-scale operation, ease of entry, labour-intensive production, reliance on indigenous resources, informally acquired skills and unregulated and competitive markets (Peattie, 1980). Hence the informal economy was defined in terms of the opposite characteristics of the formal sector and the heterogeneity of the informal sector was rarely utilized to question the supposed homogeneity of the formal sector. Moreover, underlying this early research was the naive assumption that economic life fell into two distinct, separate categories.

Anxious to emphasize the unity of the economic system, a number of researchers advocated a sub-economies model. The basic approach used was to outline a three economies model of the economy comprising the formal, informal and domestic economy (Edgell and Hart, 1988). Again, a wide range of terms was used to distinguish between different types of formal and informal work and employment. Ferman and Berndt (1981) applied the terms regular, irregular and social economic activity while Rose (1985) distinguished between the official, unofficial and domestic economies. Some researchers, while adopting this three-fold model, also introduced a variety of sub-sectors. Hence Gershuny and Pahl (1981) sub-divided the social economy into household and communal types of informal economic activity while Henry (1981) employed a six-fold model based on distinctions between legal, extra-legal and illegal activities. Other researchers have adopted a fascination for colours. Hence Davies (1985) distinguished between black and blue economies while Handy (1984) differentiated between white, black, mauve and grey economies.

The conceptual difficulties associated with reaching a universal definition of the informal economy is also reflected in attempts to measure the statistical significance of informal economic activity. Basically the research falls into two broad types, those which use indirect measures and those which utilize direct measuring techniques. However, given the various definitions of informal economic activity outlined above, it is often not clear just what is being measured. Apart from the difficulties in reaching agreement over a conceptual definition of what exactly constitutes informal economic activity, substantial methodological difficulties arise over attempting to estimate the significance of activities whose *raison d'être* is to defy detection (Feige, 1989).

Indirect approaches rely on the traces of informal economic activity that seemingly appear in statistics produced for other purposes. Thomas (1988) refers to these imprints as the 'statistical fingerprints' of informal economic activity. Since these approaches utilize published data sources that have been collected for reasons unrelated to the study of the informal economy, then according to Feige (1989:27) they represent unobtrusive measures that are not 'susceptible to wilful distortion on the part of a respondent'. Macroeconomic approaches to estimating the extent of informal economic activity can be collapsed into four broad types:

1. Traces appearing in monetary aggregates;
2. Traces revealed by tax auditing and other compliance methods;
3. Traces in the form of discrepancies between income and expenditure;
4. Traces visible in the labour market.

The estimates produced by each of these measures are reviewed in the following sections.

TRACES IN MONETARY AGGREGATES

Purchasers and sellers of goods and services within the informal economy are assumed to want to leave minimal traces of their transactions and hence conduct their businesses using cash rather than other more traceable means such as credit cards and cheques. This assumption has led some economists to suggest that an increase in currency stocks and payments is likely to indicate a growth in informal economic activity. In a widely publicized article, Gutmann (1979) suggested that the size of the underground economy is reflected in an increase in the ratio of currency relative to demand deposits held with banking institutions. Using this method, Gutmann estimated that the 'subterranean' economy of the USA amounted to approximately 10 per cent of GNP in 1976. Feige (1979) proposed an alternative approach which did not limit itself to the exclusive use of currency as a measure for estimating the size of unrecorded income. Rather Feige suggested that activity in the underground economy is likely to be recorded in measures of total transactions which are nonetheless excluded from recorded income. Hence changes in the ratio of transactions to income indicate the relative size of the underground economy. Using this method, Feige (1980) estimated that the informal economy amounted to 27 per cent of official GNP in 1979.

A more sophisticated version of this approach was used by Tanzi (1982, 1983) who investigated the relationship between changes in the level of taxation and changes in the cash/money ratios. Variations on these approaches have been applied by economists in a number of European countries (see O'Higgins, 1989 for the UK; Langfeldt, 1989 for the Federal Republic of Germany; Contini, 1989 for Italy; Barthelemy, 1989 for France). These monetary methods generally assume that transactions in the informal economy are usually (though not exclusively) paid in cash.

The monetary methods in many cases produce high estimates of the size of the informal economy. Most of these studies also indicate a significant increase in the informal economy during the 1970s. According to Feige (1979), the informal economy in the United States amounted to 19 per cent of GNP in 1976 but by 1979 this had risen to over 28 per cent. Similarly Gutmann (1979) estimated the size of the informal economy in the United States as 10 per cent of GNP in 1976 rising to over 13 per cent of GNP in 1979. However, studies utilizing these methods in other European countries have not produced such high estimates. O'Higgins (1989) estimates the size of the UK's informal economy at a more conservative 5 per cent of GNP.

TAX AUDITING AND OTHER COMPLIANCE METHODS

A number of estimates on the size of the informal economy focus on tax evasion as a primary indication of the significance of informal economic activity although as Tanzi (1982) warns even if there were no taxes, there would still be an informal economy because of various government restrictions on the activities of economic agents. In addition to tax evasion, Molefsky (1982) suggests that there are two further reasons why some individuals may participate in the informal economy. The first is to avoid losing government benefits and the second is to circumvent regulations and licensing requirements. It should also be noted that not all participants in the informal economy owe taxes. Molefsky (1982) indicates that many people's income in the United States is so low that they do not have any federal income tax liability while Hakim (1992) produces similar conclusions for the United Kingdom by listing a whole range of groups commonly thought to be active in the informal economy who are in fact legally employed workers who are not entitled to make any tax payments because of their extremely low wage rates. Moreover, some activities such as household or domestic activities are unconcerned with evading taxes and hence are excluded from these types of approaches into the extent of the informal sector.

In the United States, the research focuses almost exclusively on income tax evasion while in European countries, analyses are often extended to include evasion of social security taxes and value added taxes. The concern here is mainly on tax evasion. In the United States, the Internal Revenue Service (IRS) analyses unreported legal source income and unreported illegal-source income. The discussion here is limited to unreported legal source income. Information on this practice is derived from the IRS Taxpayer Compliance Measurement Programme (TCMP). This programme subjects a probability sample of approximately 50 000 individual income tax returns to a thorough audit examination. Using this approach, the informal economy in 1976 was estimated at between 5.9 per cent and 7.9 per cent of GNP (Tanzi, 1982). Witte (1987) suggests that unreported taxable incomes are usually generated in small scale enterprises and by the self-employed rather than by large corporations. He supplies figures for 1981 which indicate that unreported income for the first two categories amounted to $90 billion whereas unreported income for large corporations amounted to approximately $10 billion. This is because small scale enterprises and the self-employed have more opportunities to disguise the extent of their incomes compared to more regulated and bureaucratic large scale corporations.

Frey and Pommerehne (1982) quote a range of research from a number of European countries which indicate discrepancies between the aggregate amount of income in the national accounts and the aggregate income estimates based on adjusted tax returns. Macafee for the UK estimated the discrepancy at 3 per cent of GNP in 1978, Albers produced a figure of 8.9 per cent of GNP for the Federal Republic of Germany in 1968, Roze calculated an even larger discrepancy for France at 23 per cent of GNP in 1965 and this high figure was borne out by research for Italy by Campa and Visco for 1972.

The extent to which tax auditing differs from one country to another makes comparisons difficult (see OECD, 1978, 1980). Moreover, this approach generally relies on income tax returns, hence people who do not fill in such returns are left out of the analysis. This also makes it difficult to evaluate changes in the size of the informal economy over time as the estimates are grossly affected by changes in detection methods, tax structure and tax legislation (Frey and Pommerehne, 1982).

DISCREPANCIES BETWEEN INCOME AND EXPENDITURE

While income earned by an individual may go unreported or under-reported, much of it will later show up as expenditure. Hence, one way of estimating the size of the informal economy is to look at any discrepancies that might exist between income and expenditure. The underlying assumption here is that while some people may well try to hide their 'real' income when interviewed in government surveys, they will not be as concerned to conceal their expenditure. Thomas (1990) outlines discrepancies between spending and income analysed by Dilnot and Morris using Family Expenditure data for the UK. They conclude that between 10 per cent to 15 per cent of households might have some form of concealed income but that the total amount involved was not large, representing only about 2 per cent to 3 per cent of GNP. They also suggest that the self-employed were the group most likely to conceal their true income. These conclusions are echoed by O'Higgins (1980) who concludes that private households headed by self-employed persons for the UK did not report £2.10 billion in their answers to consumer surveys and by Smith (1986) who suggests that the self-employed have more scope to engage in informal economic activity. Using the 1982 Family Expenditure Survey, Smith estimates that the self-employed understated their income by as much as 20 per cent. Smith and Wied-Nebbeling (1986) in a comparison of Britain and Germany also found that in both countries, the self-employed were the group most likely to conceal part of their earnings. However, this approach has many shortcomings (see Frey and Pommerehne 1982 for a discussion of the difficulties in using this method) and the resulting estimates on the size of the informal economy need to be treated with caution.

TRACES IN THE LABOUR MARKET

A number of methods have been used to estimate the potential size of the labour force employed informally. One of the most widely used in the United States concerns comparing the Census Bureau's Current Population Survey estimate of the number of jobs and job holders with the Bureau of Labor Statistics' survey of establishments of all sizes to determine the number of people on the official payroll. The assumption behind comparing the two sets of statistics is that those working in the informal economy will declare themselves as job holders in the household survey but may not appear on the books of business enterprises. Hence, the discrepancy between both sets of figures is taken to indicate the size of the unofficial labour force. However, Mattera (1985) warns that there is no guarantee that informal workers will declare themselves as employed on household surveys. Moreover, an individual working in the regular, formal economy but with a second job in the informal economy need only acknowledge the regular job to be counted as employed, hence the second, informal job may remain hidden (Molefsky, 1982). Similarly, workers with two regular jobs in the formal economy may be counted twice thus inflating the official employment rate. Because of these reasons, the basis on which such comparisons rest is very dubious.

Portes and Sassen-Koob (1987) use small-scale business activity as a indicator of potential informal economic activity. They suggest that labour intensive industries utilizing technology that easily lends itself to piece rate dissolve into smaller and smaller enterprises. These enterprises often use informal rather than formal labour as concealment is easier for small-scale enterprises and union control is often less rigid. Large firms subcontract to small ones and these in turn subcontract to even smaller ones right down to the work-at-home level. Hence a number of researchers view an increase in small-scale businesses as evidence of a likely increase in the employment of an informal labour force. This link has been made by Contini (1982) for Italy, Lozano (1989) for the United States and Benton (1990) for Spain.

Another approach concerns the search for unaccountable increases or decreases in the official labour force. Italy provides an interesting case study to illustrate this approach. Italian interest in the informal economy emerged from an inexplicable decline in the overall labour force participation rate during the 1960s and early 1970s (Contini, 1982). During the 1950s, the official overall participation rate stood at 45 per cent. By the late 1960s, it had declined to 39 per cent while by the mid 1970s the rate had dropped to 35 per cent which was far below the rate of all of Italy's neighbours. Some researchers suggested that the decline in the official labour force participation rate was largely due to increasing segments of the working age population holding unrecorded jobs in the informal economy. The participation rates estimated by ISTAT (Italian National Income and Product Accounts Authority) were subsequently revised to try to take account of the unofficial labour force. For example, National Income Accounts were revised upward by 10 per cent to take account of the productivity of workers in small-sized firms that had been artificially under-represented in the accounting procedures. ISTAT has subsequently produced a number of estimates on the irregular labour force including multiple job holders and homeworkers and according to Blades (1982), Italy's national accounts cover a higher proportion of undeclared activities than most of the other industrial countries of the western world.

All of the above methods have been used to estimate the size of the informal economy in Europe. However, because of the conceptual and methodological difficulties involved in attempting to define and then measure informal economic activity, cross-national comparisons become very difficult as often different approaches are measuring different things. Nonetheless the OECD (1986) and the European Commission (Final Synthesis Report, 1990) have made a number of observations on the extent and significance of informal economic activity throughout Europe. In most northern European countries the informal economy is likely to represent 5 per cent or less of the level of declared work. This figure is likely to be somewhat higher for France and Belgium while in southern European countries, the figure is likely to reach 20 per cent. However as Williams and Windebank (1995) point out, none of these measures tell us anything about who is likely to be working informally (other than make assumptions that the self-employed are likely to have more opportunities to work informally). They also cannot discern local or regional variations in informal economic activity.

DIRECT MEASURES OF THE INFORMAL ECONOMY

Direct measures of informal economic activity have attempted to overcome the shortcomings of indirect approaches. These studies have been less concerned with measuring the monetary significance of the informal economy and more concerned with attempting to find out how or why certain individuals, households or localities decide to become involved in informal economic activity. The most perceptive sociological studies have used a variety of research methods to provide a comprehensive account of the social significance of such work. Ferman and Berndt's research (1981) into informal economic activity in Detroit combined a survey and ethnographic approach. Howe (1990) utilized participation observation, in-depth interviewing and data on local labour market opportunities derived largely from surveys in each area under investigation. Pahl and Wallace (1985) built up extensive knowledge of the Isle of Sheppey through participant observation and semi-structured interviews before commencing a survey of the area. They also conducted follow-up interviews with selected households in order to describe the actual patterns of work of the unemployed. However, such approaches are not without difficulties. Often they rely on specific case studies and this makes it difficult to utilize their findings for comparative purposes. My research into informal economic activity in Belfast

(Leonard, 1994) produced findings that contradicted much of the existing research into the informal economy in Britain and Ireland emphasizing the importance of locality differences in accounting for variations in opportunities and motivations to participate in informal economic activity. This point is reiterated by Edgell and Hart (1988:13) who state that 'the diversity of formal work is more than matched by the diversity of informal work, therefore theories about the social significance of particular types of informal work in specific localities would seem to be more appropriate than theories about informal work in general. Thus some forms of informal work may be expanding in one society at the same time that other forms are declining in another'.

Apart from the difficulties in using such studies for comparative purposes, direct approaches to estimating the extent and significance of the informal economy also throw up a number of methodological issues in that they often rely on individuals admitting to activities which they are attempting to conceal for tax or welfare purposes. While Lee (1993) makes a number of valid suggestions for de-sensitizing these issues, the possibility remains that individuals will not respond truthfully to attempts to uncover such activities and hence the results of these research strategies need to be treated with caution.

An amalgamation of direct and indirect approaches have been used to attempt to estimate the value of the non-monetary sector of the economy relating mainly to non-market production of goods and services in the household and subsistence agriculture. Time budget surveys have been utilized in a number of countries to estimate the amount of time spent by household members in different types of household production (see for example Gershuny and Miles, 1985, Chadeau, 1985). Often these studies are concerned with placing a monetary value on unpaid household production using an opportunity cost and market cost evaluation. The first approach attempts to measure the value of lost market income that results from production activities within the household while the second estimates the value of household production activities at corresponding market wage rates if formally paid workers from outside the household were employed to produce the goods and services involved (Feige, 1989). Murphy (1982) suggests that in 1978, the non-market sector ranged from between 37 per cent to 51 per cent of the market economy in the United States.

ACCOUNTING FOR THE INTEREST IN THE INFORMAL ECONOMY

The fact that the informal economy received such extensive coverage in developed western economies during the 1970s is an interesting phenomenon in itself and one that merits some attention. During the 1970s, the United States and many European countries were plagued with high rates of inflation, unacceptable levels of unemployment, slowed growth and declining productivity. The simultaneous occurrence of inflation and recession baffled economists and called into question the conventional macroeconomic theories on which economists based their economic predictions (Feige, 1989). It was during this period that interest turned to the potential size of unrecorded economic activity and the high estimates provided by Gutmann (1979) and Feige (1979) sparked off a wave of government and academic research on the extent and significance of the informal economy. This research was accompanied by a wide range of anecdotal evidence which seemed to suggest that huge areas of economic life escaped detection by mainstream society and its accounting procedures.

This provokes two central concerns for governments. The first is the potential loss of revenue to the state resulting from the concealment of employment. If workers are employed off-the-books or working informally and not declaring or under-declaring their income, then it is obvious that the state will be unable to collect the appropriate taxes due from such individuals. States need such revenue to fund among other things their welfare schemes and provisions. This leads on to a second main concern for governments and that is that some of those claiming welfare assistance from the state may be making false claims in that they may be working informally and thus inflating costly demands for welfare provision while simultaneously avoiding the payment of any relevant taxes. Much of the research outlined above has been concerned with estimating the potential extent of this hidden income.

The reliability of economic measurements is obviously important. Accurate data provide the empirical foundation for developing government policy. However, if major areas of economic life escape detection, then the nation's basic macroeconomic information system is vulnerable to systematic distortions and is likely to produce inaccurate estimates of the true state of economic affairs. Widespread concern emerged in many western industrial nations about the economic implications of a supposedly expanding informal economy particularly in relation to tax evasion and unregistered labour. Alford and Feige (1989:66–67) outline the policy consequences of ignoring the existence of informal economic activity. They are particularly concerned with shifts from the formal to the informal economy resulting in the informal sector growing at a faster rate than the formal sector. The consequences would be increased tax burdens, increased costs of regulatory compliance and a general lack of trust in government. The growth of the informal sector at the expense of the formal sector could also falsely signal the onset of a recession and this impression would be further reinforced if formally employed workers transferred to the informal sector and in the process grossly inflate the true level of unemployment. Similarly, consumer price indices would overstate the true price level of goods as this price level would be based on goods and services sold in the formal sector and would ignore the cheaper availability of goods and services in the formal sector. Since governments will respond to the distorted economic images of the formal economy due to their ignorance of the informal sector, then their subsequent misguided policies could turn these 'statistical illusions into an unpleasant reality' (Alford and Feige, 1989:67).

While Alford and Feige suggest that their analysis is supported by empirical evidence which indicates that the informal economy is substantial and expanding in many industrial, developed societies, much of the research outlined above produced much more conservative estimates of the size of the informal economy and recent studies indicate that informal economic activity is declining rather than increasing in importance. Nonetheless, economists, policy-makers and governments remain concerned about certain aspects of the informal economy. Pahl (1990) suggests that within the European context there is a concern that countries which rely on sweated labour might be able to produce goods more cheaply than countries where labour is protected, hence giving unfair advantage to countries which have relatively larger informal economies. Moreover, such countries are likely to underestimate the true level of economic activity in national accounts and might end up paying a lower contribution to EU funds compared to countries with higher levels of regular economic activity. While Pahl acknowledges that there is scant evidence to support these assumptions, nonetheless, anecdotal evidence which often inflate the size of the informal economy keep such concerns alive.

THE INFORMAL ECONOMY IN EUROPE AND THE UNITED STATES

It is clear from the preceding discussion that both direct and indirect approaches to the study of informal economic activity have their shortcomings. The indirect measures reviewed here have produced widely inconsistent estimates of the magnitude of the informal economy and tell us little about who is actually involved in the informal economy nor their motivations for participation. While direct methods relying on detailed case studies are able to shed more light on these issues, their limited scope makes it difficult to use such studies for comparative purposes. One of the purposes of this book is to indicate how particular social structures and localities shape, foster and constrain informal economic activities. While direct research approaches have many deficiencies, nonetheless they are better equipped for highlighting the uneven development of both the formal and informal economy within specific national boundaries and the differing local and regional responses to overall changes in the economy. The incorporation of certain groups into the informal economy and the economic responses of households and communities to wider structural constraints form a key part of the book and the diversity of these strategies are illustrated through examining a wide range of studies in various localities throughout the western world. The locally and regionally specific nature of these studies allow us to investigate how seemingly similar processes such as a move towards flexibility or increase in subcontracting can have particular rather than universal effects. Such an approach challenges the notion that the unemployed or women or ethnic minorities always react in the same way to the existence of informal economic opportunities. Not only do these opportunities differ from place to place but so too do the motivations for various groups to become involved in informal economic activities both within and between different countries.

In reviewing a substantial number of studies into the informal economy in different regions and countries, it seems clear that there are few intrinsic characteristics associated with informal economic activity. Rather, the boundaries of state regulation often determine what is formal economic activity and what is not. Since the rules governing economic activity may differ from one state to another then so will the definition of activities to be included in estimates of the informal economy differ from one country to another. Boer

(1990) suggests that what is missing from most conceptualizations of the informal economy is the lack of attention paid to the historical development of the balance between formal and informal economic activities. It is the historical development of the shifting boundaries between the formal and informal economy which forms the framework for the remaining chapters of the book. My concern is not so much with estimating the size of the informal economy in different countries but with examining some of the broad processes in capitalist and welfare systems which give rise to informal ways of working and their specific local, regional and national effects. In order to identify and illustrate these processes, the book focuses on four main aspects of informal economic activity. These are:

1. Tax evasion by regular workers (mainly moonlighters and multiple job holders);
2. Income-earning activity by the unemployed which is not declared to the relevant authorities in case it affects entitlements to welfare benefits;
3. Informal employment of immigrants, women, children and other peripheral workers;
4. Unpaid economic activities done for the direct benefit of the household or for relatives and friends outside the household on a reciprocal basis.

At first glance this approach seems (with the exception of tax evasion by regular workers) to focus on marginal activities and hence uphold the early version of the informal economy as peripheral to the workings of the formal economy. However, the argument that I present throughout the remainder of the book is that the informal economy is an integral feature of the formal economy. As a vital component of the formal economy, the nature of informal economic activity changes and responds to transformations in the formal economy. In particular, the recent crisis in capitalism has created conditions that have spurred employers to seek cheaper and more flexible production options and this has given increased impetus to activities that take place outside the regulative reach of the formal economy.

The approach to the informal economy adopted here ignores criminal activity and instead focuses on unregulated but otherwise legal forms of economic activity. Apart from the difficulties in assessing the extent and significance of criminal activities, the main focus here is on the employment of informal workers in ways that escape monitoring and regulation by the formal state. While some individuals may be employed informally as workers for criminal enterprises, for example, employed by the Mafia, nonetheless, the emphasis of this book is on the proliferation of casual, temporary, irregular employment of otherwise law-abiding citizens. Moreover, the dubious estimates that exist in relation to criminal activity are rarely concerned with the types of employment such activity generates but with the revenue made through the trafficking of illegal goods such as drugs.

The 'creative accounting' procedures adopted by firms to lower their tax bills also lies outside the scope of the book. Instead, the focus is on strategies that firms pursue to directly reduce their labour costs by employing labour informally. This may be done directly by employing labour off-the-books or indirectly by subcontracting parts of the production process out to others who may adopt dubious hiring strategies including putting work out further to homeworkers who operate invisibly from within their homes.

The following chapters outline these changes in greater detail and focus on the interplay between the labour supply of once considered peripheral workers such as women, children and immigrants and the development of bureaucratic states with increasingly elaborate tax, labour and welfare regulations. Informal workers play a fundamental role in the strategies of capital accumulation pursued by modern employers and firms. These strategies include attempts to bypass state regulation and enhance flexibility while lowering costs through the incorporation of informal workers into the economy. These informal workers are often invisible workers since they are incorporated into the economy in ways that avoid state detection and regulation.

3 Continuities and Discontinuities in Work and Employment

In order to understand current transformations in work and employment and their implications for the informal economy, it is necessary to consider the historical development of regulative systems. Economic activities only become informal within the context of formality. As states became increasingly involved in the bureaucratic control and definition of economic activity they set up distinctions between economic and non-economic activity and between work and employment. These regulatory systems are by no means universal hence the same economic practice may be part of the formal economy in one country and relegated to the informal economy in another. This is not to suggest that a clear cut distinction exists between formal and informal economic activity so that economic action falls specifically into one or the other. The formal and informal are sectors of the one economy and divisions between the two are often blurred rather than clear cut. Nonetheless, as regulatory systems developed, nation states adopted sophisticated accounting systems for placing activities for tax and welfare purposes into one category or the other and in the process set up formal divisions between work and employment. Individuals came to be recognized and defined as employed or unemployed and work became increasingly equated with formal paid employment. If people paid tax and insurance they were categorized as working, if not they were simplistically defined as economically inactive. Hence work, employment and unemployment became political constructs.

We might question whether this is the best way to define work as it seems to ignore the economic value of any work which takes place outside the formal economy. Such an approach would undermine women's significant contribution to the economy mainly in ways which lie outside this limited definition. This may lead us to suggest that the crucial distinction is one of payment. Employment is essentially market orientated and carried out for a customer or employer for money. Work is economic activity which is unpaid and involves a diverse range of activities including domestic work within the household, voluntary work and the exchange of goods and services in kind rather than cash. However, this division is problematic. Firstly, it necessitates distinguishing between work and non-work. Should all unpaid activities be characterized as work? What about the individual who grows vegetables for the family's consumption and defines his activity as a leisure pursuit. Do we define the activity as work or leisure? What weight does the actor's own meaning carry in arriving at wider definitions of what constitutes work and what does not?

We might suggest that work should be limited to activities which have a market value but every conceivable activity could in theory have a market value. Moreover, work is essentially a social phenomenon rather than solely related to market forces and economic rationality. For example, inviting one's work colleagues who are also friends to dinner where the conversation inevitably turns to issues related to work makes the distinction between work and leisure very hazy. A multitude of examples could be put forward to illustrate the difficulties in separating work from non-work and from leisure. The main point I am making in this chapter is that the crucial issue relates to the ways in which individuals, groups or states secure the power and resources to have their own interpretation of work accepted as the legitimate interpretation (Grint, 1991). Such an approach entails a historical consideration of the process whereby formal employment came to be regarded as work par excellence.

Harding and Jenkins (1989) suggest that employment is a technical term which refers to a relationship specific to a capitalist economic system. This capitalist employment relationship can be formally or informally organized and this in turn is related to the presence or absence of bureaucratic or state regulation. It makes sense then that unemployment only becomes meaningful in a context dominated by the employment relationship. Hence unemployment is not a category that would be recognized outside a very limited space and period of time (Grint, 1991). Work is more difficult to categorize. It is clear that work means more than simply employment yet it is also clear that for the concept of work to have any meaning it must not be so broadly defined as to lose any explanatory value. Work does not have an objective discrete existence of its own. Like employment, it depends on the social, economic and political relations within which it is undertaken. While these relations may take a different form and significance in different countries, nonetheless, a historical outline of how work became separated from employment reveals a number of key processes.

In order to highlight these processes and their implications for the informal economy, I have focused on the impact of the historical process of industrialization on contemporary patterns of work and employment. Since my intention is to provide a brief synopsis of what I consider to be significant issues for the resilience and development of informal economic practices, only some features can be highlighted. Lack of space precludes a thorough coverage of twentieth century transformations of work for one country much less in several countries. The limited history that is covered in the chapter has been deliberately selected to illustrate the continuities as well as the discontinuities in informal patterns of work and employment across time and space.

Four main historical processes are evident. The first concerns the emergence of regulatory systems for monitoring economic activity and the subsequent emphasis on paid employment as the primary defining characteristic of work. The second concerns the development of mass production methods such as Fordism and their implications for formal and informal types of employment. The third is the development of welfare states and their ramifications for the economic strategies pursued by individuals, households and communities. The fourth and final phase is the world-wide recession and its impact on the trend towards decentralization and flexible specialization. While these historical processes have varying regional and national effects, the aim of the chapter is to extract some common themes from these processes and to examine in particular their consequences for informal economic activity.

SEPARATING WORK FROM EMPLOYMENT

People have different motivations for engaging in productive labour. Some may do so to fulfil individual and family needs. Others may want to earn money or may be provoked by some sense of duty or obligation. Others still may view work as a vehicle for self expression or simply enjoy engaging in active labour. Indeed, most people are likely to be motivated by a variety of considerations and to participate in a variety of work practices within and outside paid employment. Certain types of work and employment are likely to become more important than others at specific stages of the life cycle. Work and employment opportunities are also conditioned by structural characteristics such as age, class, ethnicity and gender. Advances in technology, employers' demands and strategies, local, national and global development may also have an impact on the development or resilience of certain types of economic activity over others. Attempting to unravel the complexities of these issues necessitates examining the gradual separation of work from employment. This in turn is linked to the emergence and development of regulatory systems to monitor economic activity. The expansion of these regulatory systems paved the way for the establishment of a myriad of informal economic activities that escaped regulation and challenged the artificial boundaries that emerged between work and employment. According to Mingione (1990a), industrial societies developed their regulatory characters through a long phase stretching from the 1880s to the late 1960s. This period was characterized by the emergence of the male breadwinner, the collective mass worker and the concepts of employment and unemployment (Pahl, 1988). While these processes did not occur uniformly throughout western industrial nations, nonetheless, they provide a useful backdrop against which to examine the divergence forms of work and employment that emerged during this period.

Throughout the twentieth century, work became synonymous with employment and defined as the formal production and exchange of goods and services for money. However, employment is but one form of work and a brief look at the significance of work in pre-industrial times reminds us of the fallacy of deflating definitions of work to a limited set of remunerated tasks. In pre-industrial society, work was as much a social as a material activity. The social significance of work is demonstrated in the studies of classic anthropologists. Malinowski (1984) illustrated how social obligations provided the primary motivation for engaging in economic production and work and leisure were fused together in a complex web of social and economic relationships. Sahlins (1972) found that many hunting and gathering tribes engaged in the minimum amount of economic production necessary to fulfil family needs and once these had been reached, the incentive to engage in further productive labour ceased.

The social significance of work is also reflected in the economic transition of western industrial societies. Hobsbawm (1964) suggested that the working class had more important pursuits than working hard for someone else's profits. Thus, even where living conditions were austere and income low, individuals did not willingly engage in formal productive labour to alleviate their situations. While households in England had some form of access to erratic paid labour stretching back eight hundred years, nonetheless Malcolmson (1988) argues that attempts to formalize wage labour in the late seventeenth and early eighteenth century were met by widespread resistance. Selling all of one's labour power for a wage earned outside the household was regarded with suspicion by most individuals. Households preferred to implement a complex mix of work strategies both within and outside the household rather than rely on one form of economic activity.

Embarking on a range of economic strategies outside contractual wage-employment promoted self-reliance and independence and provided households with a greater level of security than could be gained through reliance on one specific economic practice. Men, women and children were all productive members of households and few households could sustain their economic needs through the formal economic activity of male members. While in the early stages of the transition from pre-industrial to industrial society, men, women and children were brought into contractual wage-employment, by the beginning of the twentieth century, the male breadwinner supporting his 'dependent' family had emerged in Britain. The household became defined simplistically as a unit of consumption rather than production and work outside employment became devalued and often rendered invisible in the state accounting procedures which emerged.

Of course, this pattern was not replicated in other European countries. In Southern Italy, Spain, Greece and Ireland in particular, traditional patterns of work persisted well into the twentieth century and co-existed with the modern forms of production that emerged in the post-war period (Mingione, 1990a). In rural areas, small-scale production, handicraft industries, petty trade and tourism provided sporadic employment and income additional and complementary to the economic gains made through agricultural labour (Hadjimichalis and Vaiou, 1990). In agriculture, employers were often family members drawing on the unpaid labour of women and children. In this instance, compliance with regulations was often non-existent and because of the fragmentary nature of such work practices, state employment laws were almost impossible to enforce. Indeed, within Southern European countries, regulative systems have been less effective than in the USA and Northern European countries. As a result, workers in the former move more frequently from employment to unemployment than in the latter. Periods of formal paid employment are accompanied by bouts of unemployment and many households continue to implement a blend of formal and informal work and employment strategies.

The US experience provides a further interesting contrast to the transition from pre-industrial to industrial patterns of working that occurred in European countries. America had to cope with transforming the work cultures of individuals from a variety of European countries. This resulted in a continual tension between native and immigrant workers and both initially resisted incorporation into the formal types of employment that accompanied the development of industrial capital. Gutman (1988) focused on two time periods in American history, the years before 1843 when factories and machinery were still new to America and the period between 1893–1917 when America became the world's industrial colossus, in order to illustrate the pressures involved in assimilating native and immigrant workers to the ethos of industrial capitalism. The first-generation mainly native American factory workers before 1843 brought irregular and undisciplined work practices into the emerging factory system. Absenteeism and drunkenness were common and Gutman quotes a range of historical sources to illustrate the unwillingness of first-generation factory workers to conform to the regularities demanded by emerging manufacturers. First-generation immigrant factory workers between 1893–1920 fared little better bringing a host of pre-industrial work habits into the factory system. While by 1894, America led the field in manufacturing, the transformation in working habits was by no means complete. Owners of competitive industry faced an uphill struggle to regulate wage labour and traditional customs persisted. Adherence to a diverse range of rituals, festivals and feasts by Italian, Irish, Greek and other immigrants conflicted with employers' attempts to improve efficiency and cut labour costs. The persistence of pre-industrial work attitudes and commitment to ethnic subcultures ensured that the transformation to industrialization had as many continuities as discontinuities for many of the diverse native and immigrant groups involved (Smelser, 1959).

Nonetheless formal employment became a central feature of the industrial economy of many western nations and while many forms of economic activity outside formal employment persisted, they increasingly became devalued as non-work or economically unproductive. It was also during this period that the concept of 'unemployment' first received formal recognition and was subjected to theoretical scrutiny (Garraty, 1978). The distinctions that gradually emerged between work, employment and unemployment indicate the interplay between the state and the economy. This is not to say that in pre-capitalist times, the state and the economy were two separate entities. Block (1994) cautions against such an approach arguing that nineteenth century theorists and their contemporary followers have wildly overestimated the discontinuity between precapitalist and capitalist societies. In both frameworks, states played a crucial role in shaping economic activity so that in both time periods the economy was essentially structured by state action. While the transition from precapitalist to capitalist society in some instances opened up more and more activities to market forces, in other cases, some markets ceased to exist, at least formally. For example, by the end of the nineteenth century, most developed market economies restricted the use of child labour, transferring many forms of the practice to the less regulated informal sector of the economy.

According to Tilly (1975), with the rise of the nation state in Western Europe, a new type of bureaucratic administrative organization came into being. This new type of state structure was capable of exercising much more power than previous states had and controlling the economic livelihood of its citizens and competing economically with other states became crucial responsibilities. In order to ensure a continual source of revenue, states organized specific economic frameworks and encouraged economic growth. On the other hand, some theorists argue that the state played a secondary role to the economy in facilitating the transfer from precapitalist to capitalist society. This approach finds expression in many classic works from Adam Smith to Karl Marx and the Adam Smith version dominates many contemporary economists' views of modernity. The transition into the modern world transpired when efficient capitalist markets evolved and could function freely (Hamilton, 1994).

Rather than viewing economies and states as two separate entities, Block (1994) suggests that researchers should focus on some of the specific ways in which both spheres intersect and then examine the variations in these intersections across time and space. Such an approach can fruitfully capture historic variations in the ways these intersections are organized. Of particular interest here are the ways in which states establish obligations and responsibilities between employers and employees. States played an active role in managing compromises between capital and labour throughout the twentieth century. The establishment of various degrees of welfare provision in different states had a fundamental impact on individual availability for paid employment and subsequent employment relationships both within and outside formal employment. These are discussed further below.

State tax policies also fundamentally shaped the employment relation. Beginning with the head taxes European colonists imposed on indigenous people to draw unwilling subsistence workers into formal paid employment, states developed taxation policies to fund their increasing involvement in the compromises secured between labour and capital. This necessitated monitoring employment in order to ensure that appropriate taxes were paid. In the process, further distinctions were drawn between work and employment for tax purposes and a whole myriad of practices emerged whereby employers and employees attempted to offset tax responsibilities by transferring some productive activities to the unregulated informal sector. The balance between formal and informal sector activity was partly shaped by the structure of the tax system in different countries as it often conditioned the choices that individuals made about the time and effort they consigned to paid formal employment.

Variations in background rules produced different outcomes. As more and more workers were drawn into formal paid employment, particularly factory employment, a variety of styles of management emerged. From an employer's perspective, these were concerned with ensuring that workers laboured hard and conscientiously while from an employee' perspective, the issue was the extent to which managerial strategies could be resisted or transformed to suit the interests of employees. The complex mix of conflict and compromise between capital and labour resulted in obscure interweaving between employees' and employers' strategies which often blurred the distinction between work and employment.

In order to pursue these issues further, I examine one archetypal example of formal paid employment which emerged, Fordism. This paves the way for a discussion of post-Fordism as this is considered to have profound implications for the arbitrary division that exists between formal and informal employment.

MASS PRODUCTION, FORDISM AND WELFARE STATES

Putting to the side national differences for the moment and considering only the general trend, we can say that, on the whole, mass production taking place in large-scale enterprises has been a typical feature of the economy over the last century (Bagnasco, 1990). This is not to say that large-scale production simply obliterated forms of work outside employment. Well into the dawn of factory production, households remained multi-skilled drawing their livelihood from a range of paid and unpaid activities. Much employment remained small-scale and organized on a social as well as an economic footing. Tracing the development of labour markets under capitalism, Tilly and Tilly (1994) suggest that initially capitalists were reluctant to supervize, regulate and control the labour power of non-capitalists. During the early phases of capitalism, they preferred to deal with formally autonomous outworkers. However, as markets expanded and capital in form of fixed assets such as factories and machinery increased, capitalists began to make the key decisions concerning the character and allocation of work. As labour markets became increasingly regulated, capitalists created jobs in capitalist-owned premises and distinctions emerged between work, employment and unemployment. Backed by law and state power, capitalists became 'creators, managers and advocates of labour markets' (Tilly and Tilly 1994:287). Pre-existing working relationships relying on craft workers and subcontractors were gradually incorporated into the factory system and in the process the autonomy of middlemen was reduced and replaced by centralized hiring, surveillance and control of employees by factory owners.

Increases in production were also associated with technological development. The links between technology and industrial development are by no means clear cut. One strand of the literature emphasizes the determinant role of technology in necessitating changes in work patterns to maintain economic efficiency and technological rationality. A variant interpretation suggests that control of the workforce rather than the demands of technology was the primary factor in promoting new ways of organising labour. After all, technology was already present in many households before the transition to factory labour. In reviewing these debates, Grint (191: 57–60) suggests that a crucial issue concerns workers' motivations for engaging in productive labour. Since workers laboured to fulfil limited wants and needs, then technological advances which would enable workers to do less and less work for more or the same money was potentially disruptive to an ideology centred on expanding production. Hence, exploiting the full potential of the emerging technology required central and hierarchic control so that workers could be coerced to work when employers required them to rather than when they wanted to.

While a range of managerial styles evolved during this period, the most influential were Fordism and Taylorism. The first assembly line production system was Ford's Detroit plant set up in 1913. Work was brought to the employee through a conveyor belt and the worker's speed at completing the task was managerially and technologically controlled. At first, the Ford moving assembly line was used solely for the mass production of the Model T Ford and consumers had to be persuaded to buy invariant products. Gradually the method of production was extended into other car industries and into the manufacture of electrical appliances and other consumer goods. Productivity was raised by the adoption of Taylorism. Through his time and motion studies, Taylor developed ways of increasing production centring on an intense division of labour, the separation of conception and execution and the substitution of skilled labour by unskilled labour. The alienating conditions associated with such a production method were offset by providing workers with high wages and other incentives.

The development of welfare states should be considered against this backdrop. Fordism consisted of a continual trade-off between employers and employees and these trade-offs were often secured by welfare-state policies (Myles, 1990). Fordism depended on the availability of stable, long-term male employees willing to engage in mind-numbing repetitive tasks with little opportunities for career progression. Such compliance could only be secured through granting workers a number of concessions. These included guaranteed employment and guaranteed income throughout the life cycle and safeguards for periods of sickness and old age often dependent on prior employment performance and earnings. Wages had to be enough to reproduce the traditional nuclear family unit centred on a full-time male breadwinner with the female occupied in full-time housekeeping duties. The substantial supply of mass produced goods also needed adequate demand to function effectively and this in turn could be achieved by paying workers income at levels adequate enough to stimulate demand for mass produced goods.

The culmination of these practices in the adoption of the post-war welfare state based on Keynesian views of supply and demand were a logical element in the Fordist system of mass production and mass consumption (Esping-Andersen, 1994). Harvey (1989) and Leitner (1990) link the rise and decline of the Keynesian welfare state to the crisis in Fordism. The Keynesian state was largely legitimated by the benefits of Fordist production. However, the transition from national to global markets made the viability of nationally based state welfarism increasingly dubious (Gaffikin and Warf, 1993). These authors point out that France began the 1980s with traditional Keynesian strategies to neutralize recessionary pressure, only to retreat as the awareness of the unfeasibility of any single nation pursuing such a deliverance in an increasingly internationalized economy become apparent. By this stage, the Keynesian-welfare state began a terminal decline in a number of European countries and the US exemplified by the rise of Thatcherism in the UK and Reganism in the US.

Of course these general processes mask national differences in welfare state types and peculiarities in welfare state organizations are discussed later. The point I want to emphasize here is that even where such broad processes were most pronounced, welfare states faced a growing crisis in that the premise on which they were based – male workers in full time employment throughout most of their lives with wives engaged in household duties – is no longer the norm for any country in the western world. The mass entry of married women into the formal labour market, growing levels of unemployment and the internationalization of the division of labour have created major difficulties for the welfare state programmes developed by many western industrial countries. In attempting to deal with these crises, states have tried to dismantle, reduce or decline to implement welfare strategies and in the process opened up opportunities for informal economic activities. This crisis in welfare state policy and provision has coincided with a crisis in mass production. The long-term trend towards centralization has been stopped in its tracks by a newly emerging trend in the opposite direction. It is within this counter trend towards decentralization and flexibility that informal economic activity emerges as a central feature of the economic structures of most industrial societies as they approach the new millennium.

POST-FORDISM, DECENTRALIZATION AND FLEXIBILITY

In their book *The Second Industrial Divide* (1984) Piore and Sabel argue that the late 1960s has been characterized by a break from Fordism, mass production and product standardization. Instead economies are moving towards 'flexible specialization' whereby products are less standardized and workers' skills become more flexible. The term post-Fordism is also used to describe this transition. Economies are characterized as moving from Fordism to neo-Fordism to post-Fordism. As outlined earlier, Fordism was based on mass production and mass consumption facilitated by an extensive division of labour and alienated workers using limited skills. Neo-Fordism retained the focus on mass production and mass consumption. However, production and consumption were internationalized so that workers from developing countries could be drawn into the production and consumption process leading to rising unemployment levels in western industrial nations. Post-Fordism or 'flexible specialization' represents a split from mass production and consumption and concentrates on product specialization for specialized, often localized markets. Hence, the concept moves the focus beyond the work place and encompasses producer-customer relations (Grint, 1991).

'Flexible specialization' is distinguished from mass production by a craft form of work organization that relies on the flexible skill levels of the workforce rather than on de-skilled mass production methods. Rather than isolated workers labouring individually, team sharing is the norm particularly in times of recession. Mass markets are replaced by specialized niche markets whereby new technologies are utilized to provide smaller amounts of 'customized' products. Hence it is not so much changes in technology but changes in product markets which are responsible for these sweeping transformations (Piore and Sable, 1984).

Up to now, I have presented a very general overview of main changes in work patterns throughout the twentieth century. These broad changes mask significant regional and national differences. Even in countries such as Italy and the USA which are utilized to exemplify such processes, they are unlikely to have occurred in the linear way implied by the literature. The diversity in work patterns is obviously much more complicated than any of these models suggest and pre-Fordist, Fordist, neo-Fordist and post-Fordist strategies are likely to coexist within and across most nation states.

Jessop (1991) for example, argues that under global Fordism, not all economies had to be Fordist in all respects. To secure economic success, Jessop argues economies could follow one of two paths. Firstly, they could assume a largely Fordist dynamic with economic growth being mainly based on an expanding home market. Alternatively, they could occupy one or more key niches in non-Fordist sectors such as small batch capital goods or agriculture and fuel and satisfy mass consumption based on growing export demands. The British economy was unable to follow either path and thus its mode of growth could be regarded as 'flawed Fordism' (Jessop, 1991:138). This exposed the British economy more sharply than most to the global structural economic crisis and paved the way for the entrenchment of new right ideologies in Britain. Workers' rights came to be regarded as rigidities and costs (Minford, 1983). This led to the development of state policies to promote 'labour flexibility' based on lowering wages and weakening trade unions. The subsequent deregulation of the labour market led to the development of a wide range of precarious types of 'legal' employment (Standing, 1989).

The evolutionary general trend outlined by the literature provides a useful backdrop for examining broad trends in current patterns of work and employment and their implications for informal economic activity. Whether the processes mentioned here had pronounced or limited effects in specific nation states, it is clear that they have major implications for the interface between formal and informal economic activity. As formal employment has become more flexible and decentralized, the boundary between formal and informal employment and between work and employment has become more blurred. The remainder of the chapter highlights some of these national effects and their ramifications for the informal economy.

FLEXIBLE SPECIALIZATION

Flexibility is usually divided into two broad types; functional/internal flexibility and numerical/external flexibility. The former refers to internal flexibility within an organization and involves multi-skilling and the removal of job demarcation. This in turn may necessitate providing multi-skilled workers with improved terms and working conditions. The second represents an attempt to cope with fluctuating supply and demand through flexibility in the numbers employed and their contractual terms. This involves the use of primary and secondary labour markets to generate a mixture of core and peripheral workers. The primary labour market tends to be isolated from the competitive labour market. Employers tend to recruit individuals for certain jobs from among those who already hold other jobs in the same firm. Hence they exhibit internal labour market structures of promotion. The primary labour market tends to operate among large, profitable and capital intensive industries. The secondary labour market, by contrast, exhibits the opposite of these characteristics. It tends to be less stable than the primary labour market, offering insecure, low-skilled employment to segmented groups of workers, such as women and ethnic minorities. The workforce thus becomes divided into core and peripheral workers. Core workers enjoy relatively stable, well-paid employment while peripheral workers experience irregular, low-paid employment.

Murray (1988a) focuses on the implications of flexible specialization for the Italian workforce. In their struggle against declining profitability, Italy's dominant firms sought to restructure production through decentralization and the introduction of new technology. Decentralization provided a logical solution to two principal problems – the emergence of a militant, well organized labour movement and the stagnation of world markets. Once labour rebelled and markets began to stagnate, the efficiency of the Fordist-Taylorist mode of production was undermined. This system ultimately depended on the subordination of labour to capital. Decentralization was initially implemented as a short term strategy for diluting the advances made by the labour movement. Work which once took place in large factories was 'put out' to a network of small firms, artisans or domestic outworkers where the influence of unions was minimal. The success of the strategy in enabling capital to deal with fluctuating markets while simultaneously intensifying the labour process at minimal cost undermined motivations to recentralize production.

Murray (1988a) outlines the negative consequences for the labour force. Decentralization enables capital to reduce costs and increase labour exploitation. Putting out also enables capital to exploit sexual and racial divisions in the labour market by incorporating women and ethnic minority groups into the secondary labour market. Decentralization curbs moves to locate production in developing countries by exploiting the potentially cheap, well disciplined workforce within advanced industrial countries who can be brought in and out of the labour market through the putting out system. Murray quotes macro-data which indicates an increase in small-scale production units throughout Italy. He further suggests that this process is assisted by employment legislation whereby important parts of the Workers' Statute do not apply to firms employing fewer than 15 workers. Splitting up the work process into a number of separate small-scale units makes collective identity and organization more difficult to achieve. Workers are often invisible from one another and their employment conditions become increasingly precarious and marginalized.

Murray's account of the impact of decentralization on the workforce provides a striking contrast to Piore and Sabel's (1984) account of the positive impact of decentralization in Japan. They imply that Japanese work organization based on flexibility was essentially progressive and beneficial for the Japanese workforce. United States management consultants have tried to 'sell' these work methods to unions within the United States and European countries and often investment is linked to the implementation of Japanese strategies. However, Tomaney (1990) questions the extent to which Japanese work methods involve higher levels of skill and workforce participation and operate with workers' approval and consent as implied by Piore and Sabel. Instead, Tomaney argues that the Japanese 'economic miracle' is based on a misrepresentation of key events in Japanese labour history and a highly partial account of the real nature of work in Japan. Of particular significance were the historic defeats inflicted on militant Japanese workers organizations before and after the second world war. Hence it was the absence of independent trade unions in Japan which allowed the complete functional flexibility necessary for Japanese production methods to work. Tomaney (1990:38) points out 'the harmonious industrial relations which they (Piore and Sable) describe were won by capital in struggle against labour'. In other words, flexibility is being established on capital's terms and even in its most advanced forms does not guarantee the benefits for labour implied by its proponents.

Flexibility may take different forms in different countries and be motivated by different considerations. Grint (1991) suggests that many contemporary trade unions in Britain have pre-Fordist traditions of single skills and demarcated territories. This mode of production makes British companies less flexible than Japan. The failure to introduce and utilize the technology of flexible specialization was used by Hirst and Zeitlin (1989) to account for the relatively poor performance of UK manufacturing. By contrast, the competitive success of (West) Germany, like Japan, lay in its ability to foster a multi-skilled workforce to produce a wide range of semi-customized goods. While these trends have been reversed in recent years and some European economies are considered over-regulated and thus not doing as well as the UK and the US, nonetheless, it is clear from the above discussion that motivations to decentralize and de-regulate labour depend on a complex interplay between capital and labour. In nations where independent trade unions were absent (Japan) or relatively powerless (UK – Murray, 1988b), decentralization had a detrimental effect on employment whereas in countries where trade unions were more powerful such as (West) Germany, some limited benefits have been won for members (Wainwright, 1987).

Moreover, the incentive to introduce casual labour force attachment may also stem from different employer concerns. As pointed out earlier, Italian employers (like French employers) introduced flexibility to ward off worker militancy and to evade government and union regulations. Japan was more concerned with attempts to cope with a shortage of labour and expanding non-regular employment emerged as a device to encourage more peripheral groups into the labour market such as students, women and illegal workers. By contrast, United States employers were less concerned with evading specific rules than with responding to growing global and domestic competition by attempting to dilute workers expectations of long-term employment through the introduction of less regular forms of employment (Tilly and Tilly, 1994:299).

FLEXIBILITY AND THE INFORMAL ECONOMY

It is clear that the above trends may have a significant effect on the overall organization of work and employment. As industries adopt more flexible ways of organizing production, they encourage a growth in informal economic activity. The workforce begins to polarize as organizations concentrate on 'core' activities and full-time jobs are reserved for skilled staff earning relatively high incomes and experiencing good working conditions. Less essential services are farmed out to those with low skill levels and their future becomes one of insecure part-time or irregular employment with wages forced down by domestic and international competition (Christie, 1994). The associated trend towards small scale enterprises and high product differentiation promotes subcontracting and a concomitant growth in sweatshops and homeworking. As workers become employed either formally or informally in small scale enterprises, the collective identity of unions weakens and they become less powerful. According to Castells and Portes (1989), undermining organized labour's control over the work process is one of the fundamental goals of informalization although they remind us that this cannot be the only cause as many sectors which have undergone informalization, particularly in the service sector, were previously dominated by small scale firms and not highly unionized to begin with. Nonetheless, this trend has intensified and employers in small scale enterprises may find it easier to evade health, safety and employment laws and to employ labour off-the-books. Small enterprises provide a highly conducive setting for casual hiring, under-reporting of income and other informal practices. Moreover, very small scale firms can 'officially' close down one day and reopen the next as an underground concern. Alternatively, new businesses may use the informal sector as a tactic for testing the market and their potential economic viability and may move towards formalization once they have become established after a period of informalization. As formal employment opportunities decline or become downgraded, workers may be encouraged to engage in informal employment as and when such opportunities arise. Those who are marginalized in the formal economy such as women, children and ethnic minorities may find opportunities to sell their labour in the informal economy. Hence the informal economy often promotes the segmentation of the labour force along gender, age and ethnic lines.

Let us look at some case studies to depict the above trends. The move towards smaller scale enterprises can be illustrated by examining their presence in Spain, Italy and US. Ormerod (1994) points out a puzzling feature of the Spanish economy in that while the Spanish economy has practically doubled in size in real terms since 1970, employment is actually lower now than it was in the 1970s. This is partly because many Spanish industries from the 1970s onwards have experienced a process of decentralization. The textile and clothing industry for example is made up of small units involved in autonomous production phases. These fragmented, decentralized activities can be performed outside the factory either in private homes or in clandestine workshops. This leads to five types of informal employment (Lobo, 1990a). Firstly, legal workers in legally registered firms who may not declare the full amount of hours worked, omitting in particular, overtime. Again this reminds us that the under-reporting of income is linked to the implementation of taxation systems regulated by states. Secondly, legally registered firms may employ a proportion of their labour needs off-the-books. Thirdly, legally registered firms may employ homeworkers who remain invisible workers in terms of legal employment rights and labour market participation statistics. Fourthly, previously formally employed workers may be dismissed but given a machine as compensation and then installed at home or in a sweatshop as an informal entrepreneur fulfilling orders emanating from previous employers. Finally, some workers may be employed on short-term work contracts in small scale workshops allowing employers to gain optimal flexibility in terms of needed labour power.

Similar trends towards smaller-scale enterprises are evident in the footwear and toy-making industries of Alicante and the electronics industries in Madrid (Lobo, 1990a). In the latter instance, electronic firms retain core technical processes such as design and installation and subcontract out autonomous assembly line phases of production. The labour market itself becomes polarized around highly qualified core workers and unskilled periphery workers. Segmentation becomes more pronounced as young people and women dominate the less regulated sectors of the changing national economy.

In Northern Italy, leading firms decentralize less profitable productive activities to small scale firms and sweatshops which have recourse to irregular labour. Reporting on the prevalence of this for various regions of Italy, Mingione (1990a) stresses that in many cases, it is not the direct employer who benefits from the lower cost of informal labour but the larger enterprise at the end of the chain. This trend towards smaller scale enterprises has occurred in the textile and clothing industry and in traditional engineering and construction. In the South of Italy, various aspects of the production process are put out to several different workshops each of which assumes responsibility for finding and funding the necessary labour. The workforce commonly becomes divided into formal and informal workers. Formal workers receive a work contract which enables workers to gain minimum employment guarantees while the informal workforce labour with no such contracts or guarantees.

The process of decentralization was also assisted by the efforts of large industries to control labour power during the 1960s. This led to the implementation of new laws to reduce the tax burden on employers. Artisanal enterprises with less than fifteen workers were exempted from certain provisions of the tax code and of the statute of labour (Piore and Sabel, 1984). While in some cases, this reduced the necessity of employing labour off-the-books, for many small scale enterprises the strategy of simultaneously employing formal and informal labour provided firms with enhanced flexibility and opportunities to reduce labour costs while intensifying the work process.

In the US, Sassen (1991) identifies a number of trends responsible for the move towards smaller scale enterprises and associated informalization. Firstly, she looks at the concentration of employment into high income and low income jobs. The high income strata and the related gentrification of housing and retail markets creates opportunities for informal economic activity. Hence, demand for informal workers could never develop without a simultaneous expansion of markets for products and increased affluence of some sections of the population (Hadjimichalis and Vaiou, 1990). Residents in middle class areas often rely on informal construction workers to upgrade or maintain their housing accommodation. Non-union contractors drawing largely on the use of the informal labour of migrants commonly engage in residential construction and repairs. Quoting a survey from the Department of Buildings in 1981, Sassen (1991:88) indicates that 90 per cent of all interiors in a four block survey in Manhattan had been done without a building permit. Similarly in Portugal, the urban middle class create a demand for second houses and these construction projects are generally undertaken by small firms employing informal labour (Lobo, 1990b).

Affluent buyers also create a demand for goods and services that are not mass-produced or sold through mass outlets (Sassen-Koob, 1987). This enhances the development of customized production based on small runs and speciality items. These enterprises need to be located near to speciality markets and this in turn reverses the trend for labour intensive industries to be transferred outside major cities or located solely in self contained low-income areas within major cities.

Subcontracting becomes a key strategy in this move to customized production. Under subcontracting the distinction between the formal and informal sectors of the economy become increasingly blurred as workers move between one and the other form of employment and firms implement a complementary mix of formal and informal production strategies. Firms in the formal sector use the informal sector as part of their overall strategy to maximize profits at minimal cost. Sassen points out how the existence of a large immigrant workforce facilitates the growth of sweatshops and homeworking in New York and Los Angeles but emphasizes that informal employment does not simply represent the survival strategies of immigrants. Rather it is subtly linked to the development of advanced capitalism and the workings of the informal economy in many European countries. This widespread usage of peripheral members of the indigenous labour force in diverse economic settings indicates the fallacy of simply equating the informal economy with the traditional efforts of immigrants to get by in periods of severe economic difficulty.

Nonetheless, expanding low income populations encourages the growth of informal economic activities by enhancing demand for low cost goods and services. Sassen argues that the consumption needs of the low wage workforce are largely met by small scale retail establishments which rely on family labour and generally fall below minimum safety and health standards. Hence the parallel development of a market for high priced and low priced goods and services facilitates the trend towards informalization.

While informal economic activity is often a reaction against state regulation of the economy, it is worth emphasizing at this point that many governments often tolerate informal economic activity as a way of resolving potential social conflicts or promoting political patronage (Castells and Portes, 1989:27). Italy provides a striking example of this tacit policy. Warren (1994) examines the role of the state in shaping the structure of the informal economy in three main regions of Italy; the historically less developed South of the country, the Northwest where large-scale industry is located and 'the third Italy' which flourishes on small scale industry. He argues that the differing political arrangements in each of these regions has profound implications for informal economic opportunities. In the South of Italy, clientelism is particularly acute. This thwarted economic development in the region as local parties aided by the Mafia utilized public funds investments to strengthen patronage ties. Mafia controlled construction companies built unoccupied plants and infrastructure often relying on informal labour. Small scale firms obtain little institutional support and find it almost impossible to become independent of larger politically controlled firms. In the process, an exploitative type of informal economy flourishes in the South of Italy based on traditional, labour intensive industries producing cheap products for local markets or for export and utilizing the easily exploitable labour power of women and children.

Within 'the third Italy', the informal economy takes a much less exploitative shape. Here the formal and informal economy are very closely connected with many small-scale formal employees engaging in moonlighting in the informal economy. Small-scale firms are more independent from large-scale firms and unlike the small scale firms in the South have direct access to markets. There is also much more co-operation among small-scale firms in 'the third Italy' so that within specific regions, specialization occurs. Hence Modena specializes in knitwear while Bologna specializes in motorcycles and shoes. Each region is characterized by a number of small scale outlets, each making extensive use of informal labour.

Warren relates the strength of the informal sector in 'the third Italy' to the role adopted by local political parties in the region. 'The third Italy' is divided into the Red regions including Tuscany and Umbria ruled by the Communist Party and the White regions including Veneto and Trentino Alto Adige under the Christian Democrats. Unlike the South of Italy, the level of clientelism in 'third Italy' is relatively low. Within the Communist regions, political and social ties influence opportunities for formal and informal economic activity, but they support party and institutional power rather than the personal power networks that characterize the South. This allows the informal sector to develop characteristics similar to the small industrial formal sector rather than exist as a more exploitative appendage as in the South. As a result, opportunities and conditions in the informal economy are more lucrative than in other regions of Italy. While the White region of 'the third Italy', like the South of Italy, is ruled by the Christian Democrats, nonetheless the party pursues different objectives in each region with the party supporting rather than hindering small-business development in Central Italy. This indicates the heterogeneous nature of the political system in Italy where even the same party may adopt radically different strategies in one region compared with another profoundly influencing the nature of the informal economy in the process.

The Northwest of Italy provides a further contrast. Here the Christian Democrats developed ties with large firms resulting in a lack of support for small-scale industry. When these firms began to put out various aspects of production to small-scale enterprises, a number of sweatshops and highly exploitative informal work opportunities emerged. Warren suggests that this leads to the development of a mixed type of informal economy encompassing some of the features of the lucrative informal economy which characterizes 'the third Italy' with the more exploitative aspects of the informal economy that characterizes the South of Italy.

The reason for focusing in such depth on this case study is to counterbalance the view put forth earlier which emphasized the efforts of industry to offset the liabilities of the Fordist-welfare system as the key factor in encouraging informal economic activity. Of at least equal importance is the role of the state in promoting or hindering the development of informal economic practices. While some recent representations of the informal economy are giving increasing attention to the role of the state in the development of the informal economy, often this is at a national or international level. Warren reminds us that the state is not a single actor as implied in much of this literature. His analysis of the informal economy in Italy illustrates how the state varies regionally. In my own research in Northern Ireland, the regional policies of the Stormont Government in allocating resources to one section of the community at the expense of the other fundamentally shaped the formal and informal economic opportunities that subsequently emerged (Leonard, 1994).

Benton (1989, 1990) suggests that it is the historical legacy of a strong centralized state and subsequent weak nature of internal political alliances that inhibits the ability of the informal economy in countries like Spain to have the same potential for development as 'the third Italy'. While Italy had a strong tradition of worker co-operatives and a high degree of political co-operation among business, local government and workers in some regions, these conditions were absent in Spain. Under the Franco regime, the Spanish economy was highly regulated. The low wages that were made possible by the repression of organized labour reduced the incentives for employers to seek informal wage labourers. Although the workers' protests which emerged during the late 1960s were met by further repression, nonetheless the government responded by expanding benefits to workers including increasing wages but passed these costs largely on to employers. During this phase, the possibility of recruiting labour off-the-books became an attractive option for employers. These incentives were increased in the aftermath of Franco's death in 1975 as the legalization of labour unions soon followed.

In the wake of the economic crisis of the mid 1970s, the production process became increasingly fragmented and several phases of production were shifted underground. However, the nature of internal political alliances reduced the potential for a positive outcome of these trends. While small-scale and partially unregulated industrial enterprises flourished during this period, state policies continued to support large industry on the assumption that the benefits of this aid would eventually 'trickle down' to smaller firms.

Centralized political conditions thwarted the emergence of local or sectoral alliance building. The absence of these alliances worked against the formation of co-operatives among small-scale subcontracting firms. Benton traces this reluctance to the narrow economic interests of workers in the unions which emerged in the late 1960s and early 1970s. Once substantial wage increases had been achieved, active membership in new labour unions went into terminal decline. Moreover, co-operative movements have traditionally received little institutional support. Benton suggests that this is mainly due to the limited autonomy in industrial policy that exists within the still centralized Spanish system. Hence, unlike the successful local efforts to help industrial co-operatives in central Italy, local initiatives in Spain were hampered by lack of funding and control over tax incentives.

This has crucial implications regarding the ability of the informal economy to respond positively to changing conditions in world markets. Unlike the thriving regional development of the informal economy in Italy, in Spain, particularly in labour intensive industries such as the shoe industry, informal enterprises remained dependent on established firms and relied on a system of sweatshop labour including homeworking. Benton concludes that the persistence of strong states in many southern European countries inhibits the ability of the local level alliances to develop. These alliances are essential for providing the framework whereby informal economic enterprises can develop into viable, autonomous business enterprises that can transcend the informal and formal sector.

PERIPHERAL FORDISM

While the existence of Fordism as the reigning paradigm for industrial development had a profound influence on the subsequent
nature of flexible specialization, it is important to emphasize at
this point, that in many regions of Europe, large scale industry
never assumed the importance outlined in these earlier debates. As
the case studies outlined thus far demonstrate, very few national
economies come close to ideal-type Fordism. Rather each case
study indicates different combinations of Fordist and non-Fordist
features. In relation to France, Smith (1989) outlines how millions
of small farmers and handicraft workers co-existed with advanced
industry making France the 'country of diversity' (Friedmann, 1955).
According to Lipietz (1988), Southern European countries such as
Portugal and Greece represent a kind of 'peripheral Fordism'. It is
to an examination of these economies that we now turn.

Greece experienced a continuous growth in industrial investment
and employment throughout the 1970s and 1980s largely due to an
expanding domestic market and opportunities for export to other
EU countries. Chronaki *et al.* (1993) examine the impact of these
opportunities on Thessaloniki which is the second largest urban
area in Greece. Protectionist quotas against countries outside the
European Union benefited Thessaloniki which was able to export
'just-in-time' low cost quality goods to European markets. However, while industrial productivity rose, wage rates remained among
the lowest in Europe. This was largely related to the traditional,
rather than the new existence of small-scale firms and various forms
of atypical employment that characterized the region. These firms
often implemented illegal or semi-legal practices such as evading
taxation, social security payments, operating without a permit, viol-
ating health and safety standards and using informal labour.

Thirty-two percent of the firms surveyed by Chronaki *et al.* (1993)
operated in small, dark, damp basements without a permit. The
authors quote 'official' government estimates which suggest that in
addition to the 23 000 'official' workers in clothing and knitwear,
another 35 000 are likely to work secretly at home. Small-scale firms
and workshops rely on a flexible local labour market and tend to
operate in close geographical proximity to one another.

Despite or possibly because of these opportunities to exploit labour, Greece remains one of the weakest economies in Europe.
High inflation and national debt spiral upwards in the face of low

industrial investment and low productivity. The low wage, labour intensive sectors on which areas such as Thessaloniki depend have been hit by international competition and diminishing domestic and European demand. This has resulted in reductions in productivity despite intensification of labour. Chronaki *et al.* argue that these difficulties are likely to become more pronounced with the opening up of eastern European labour markets.

While current European policies favour local development initiatives backed by provisions to improve workers' access, Chroniki *et al.* warn that the cornerstone for survival for many small-scale enterprises in Greece is the absence of regulation and workers' acceptance of deteriorating working conditions. They conclude that images of post-Fordist workers in jobs created through technological innovation seem far removed from the reality of many Greek people's working lives.

Portugal is another region where the Fordist model has never been fully developed. The country is characterized by low levels of basic infrastructures, a weakly developed welfare state, small numbers of large firms and a lack of well developed local economic groupings (Syrett, 1993). Like Greece, the historical development of Portugal was based on a highly centralized regime with weak local government structures. Syrett suggests that the economy transformed from 'primitive Taylorism' based on a low wage export economy towards 'peripheral Fordism' based on increased import-substitution production. Portugal became integrated into the world economy in a dependent manner relying on imports for about 80 per cent of its food requirements (despite the fact that about one fifth of its population is involved in agriculture) and exporting a narrow range of manufacturing goods produced by labour intensive, low wage industries.

Labour markets in Portugal were traditionally characterized by a high level of flexibility and informal working arrangements represent a crucial aspect of the overall economy. Throughout the 1970s, traditional industries based on low-cost, flexible labour expanded creating an increased number of unstable, low-skilled jobs. Vulnerable groups such as women, the young and the old have been incorporated into the labour market, often in highly exploitative ways. The proportion of the population located outside the formal labour market continued to expand throughout the 1980s. Yet despite high growth rates throughout this period, the Portuguese economy remains structurally weak. Syrett (1993) attributes this to

Portugal's continued dependence on the wider international economy which continues to produce uneven internal development and impedes the ability of small scale informal ventures to implement autonomous modes of development. These case studies demonstrate the importance of local government structures and policies in facilitating or thwarting the positive economic potential of the informal economy.

INFORMAL ECONOMIC OPPORTUNITIES AND PRACTICES

Much of the literature outlined in the previous section has generally been utilized to examine the changing nature of formal employment and is thus often excluded in the debate concerning the informal economy. Yet, if we accept the general premise that the formal and informal economy are inextricably related, then it seems obvious that profound changes in the structure of formal employment will have major implications for the informal sector. There are a number of other ways in which the formal and the informal economy are connected. Motivation to employ labour informally is closely associated with attempts by capital to avoid state regulation with regard to enforcement of safety, employment and insurance legislation and compliance with collective bargaining agreements. Hence, government regulations impose costs on formal businesses that in turn attempt to bypass these constraints. Hadjimichalis and Vaiou (1990:83) refer to this as 'profitably exploiting the inadequacies of the formal regulatory system'. They point out that in the Southern European countries of Spain, Portugal, Italy and Greece, many enterprises under-declare the value of their production or sales in order to avoid tax payments. Where companies operate at an international level, over-pricing imports and under-pricing exports can lead to internal price fixing which enables companies to avert their full tax obligations. Hence, the state through its attempts to regulate the economy through tax policies and other measures actively encourages the development of informal ways of working.

The rise of the welfare state in the post-war period may have also promoted the development of the informal economy as companies may hire informal labour to avoid its reach. During the recessionary periods which have characterized advanced economies since the 1970s, the increases in taxes necessary to pay for the various social benefits achieved under the beacon of the welfare state make compliance extremely economically burdensome. Of course some states have attempted to respond to this situation by dismantling their welfare state and legally deregulating the peripheral workforce. Hence, in the UK for instance, temporary, part-time and casual employment has been legally deregulated reducing the incentive to employ labour informally. This legal tolerance for atypical types of employment means that various forms of work which in other regulatory systems are informal are perfectly legal and formal in the British context. Often there is little incentive not to declare such work practices as in many instances they are exempt from taxation and other legal obligations (Mingione, 1994a). In other countries, particularly in Southern Europe with ineffective welfare provision and the survival of large areas of traditional activities, states may turn a blind eye to participation in the informal economy as a way of compensating for the inadequacies of formal provision for peripheral groups.

States may also tolerate informal ways of working in their attempts to compete in the international arena. The emergence and development of neo-Fordism whereby mass production was transferred to third world countries utilizing cheap, docile labour led to the widespread entrenchment of unemployment in many advanced economies. While 'third world' countries have traditionally informalized themselves in order to secure international contracts, it is only recently that such tactics have become a prominent feature of developed economies. Pockets of low-wage immigrant and indigenous peripheral workers allow western firms to compete with 'third world' factories. In Portugal, for example, the widespread existence of informal labour enables Portuguese exports to compete favourably with other European countries in the international market. Similarly in parts of Spain and Italy where there is only one industrial activity and where small scale enterprises are dominant, the orientation may be towards the international market and to promote competitiveness, governments may ignore non-compliance with the regulatory procedures in existence. Hence, tolerance by national governments of breaches in formal employment and production legislation enables peripheral countries like Portugal to cope more easily with the effects of international world-wide recession (Lobo, 1990b).

Employing labour off-the-books also facilitates capital's attempts to escape the regulatory arm of the state. As outlined previously, the move towards flexible specialization promotes this process as it encourages a growth in small-scale businesses which often find it easier to operate informally. As large firms 'put out' the peripheral aspects of the production process to small autonomous units, they encourage the growth of sweatshops and homeworking which often depend on the informal labour power of individuals. Chapter 4 outlines in detail the characteristics of workers who engage in informal types of employment, hence only the general trends influencing the supply of informal wage labour are outlined here.

While all kinds of workers participate in the informal economy and while the income gained can sometimes exceed the amount that could be made through formal employment, nonetheless, informal economic practices tend to attract those in a weak position in the formal labour market on the basis of age, gender and ethnicity. Hence, immigrants, ethnic minority groups, the young, the old and women tend to be over-represented among the ranks of informal wage labourers. The increase in unemployment levels throughout many European countries and the United States has paved the way for the development of informal ways of working and enhanced motivations to engage in informal economic activity in the absence of viable alternatives. This has been accompanied by a decrease in regular stable jobs so that even those with access to formal employment may have to engage in informal economic activity to cope with the insecurity of their formal employment or decline in real wages. Many countries faced with the recession of the 1970s have had to introduce austerity measures which have led to a fall in the value of wages and encouraged a growth in moonlighting and second job holding often in the informal sector of the economy. In all of these respects, the trend towards informalization enables those most affected by economic recession to achieve some element of economic security.

Of course, households have also to adopt to changing local, national and international economic environments. Up to now the focus has been on the various forms of informal employment generated by the transformations in production and consumption in the formal economy. In presenting a brief outline of the transformation from pre-industrial to industrial society, I have suggested that this was accompanied by a growing movement away from unwaged labour to formal and informal employment. But of course this break was never complete in any country in the advanced world and many households continued to implement mixes of paid and unpaid economic activity. Smith (1990), outlining the economic strategies of working class households in the United States, suggests that the post war period was characterized by an intensification of Fordism based on increasing the wages available to households to enable them to buy the mass products generated by Fordism. However once the recession of the 1970s began to bite, this strategy ran into terminal difficulties. As real wages fell in value, the need for additional household members, mainly women, to enter wage labour became essential to maintain household expenditure on consumer durables. Fordism also penetrated the household in the form of the mass consumer durables produced by this production method. These gadgets, according to Smith, are often inappropriately regarded as labour saving gadgets aimed at assisting the entry of women into formal paid employment by reducing their involvement in unpaid household labour. However, Smith outlines the considerable work involved in utilizing these gadgets and the gradual disappearance of alternatives. If we take personal laundry for instance, in 1909, 60 per cent of working class families sent out a proportion of their laundry needs to commercial laundry services (Smith, 1990:125). Automatic washing machines and dryers not only eradicated this trend but in the process commercialized the washing of clothes in a variety of ways through the production of a wide range of detergents and ironing aids to the development of a whole new branch of the textile industry in the form of synthetic fabrics geared to maximize the advances of home laundry methods. This formal substitution of once informally rendered services did not lead to a significant reduction in household labour as Smith quotes figures to indicate that between 1920 and 1968 households increased by half an hour per week their involvement in laundry work. Smith's main point is that Fordism assisted the transformation of the internal workings of households by bringing previously unwaged household members into the labour market in order to maintain the household's purchasing power in times of recession. While in the process, Fordism helped eradicate precapitalist forms of unwaged labour; it called into being new forms of unwaged household labour essential to the development of the process of commodification which characterizes advanced capitalist economies.

These issues are explored in more detail in Chapter 5 where the internal workings of the household are the primary focus. Informal work is often structured within household strategies. As goods and services once supplied by the formal economy are transferred

to the household, new forms of unwaged labour emerge or traditional ways of getting by within households persist or take on greater
economic significance. Households become self-provisioning units,
drawing on the informal labour supply of family members, and the
communities in which households are located become locations for
the development of reciprocal economic transactions as households
attempt to maintain some form of economic security in an increasingly insecure and changing economic environment.

CONCLUSION

In this chapter I have presented a brief overview of the main trends
that have shaped transformations in the world of work, employment and unemployment over the last century. Broadly speaking,
the literature suggests that the transformation from pre-industrial
to industrial society was accompanied by a widespread movement
of work from the household to the factory system. While this process was more pronounced in some countries than in others, nonetheless as the twentieth century progressed, divisions emerged in
most advanced industrial economies between work and employment.
Work came to be defined as formal paid employment and other
forms of economic activity that fell outside this limited definition
were marginalized and ignored in statistical accounts of economic
activity in most advanced states. Industrialization in the United States
and Europe created what has come to be called Fordism based on
large scale assembly line production. The economic troubles of the
1970s and 1980s resulted in this method of production coming under
increasing criticism and flexible specialization emerged as a strategy to enable crisis ridden economies to react to continuous change
(Pedersen *et al.* 1994).
    This notion of a simplistic linear progression from work to changing
types of formal employment was challenged in the chapter by emphasizing the importance of outlining the historical development
of regulative systems in order to enhance our understanding of the
arbitrary division that exists between the formal and the informal
economy. This historical approach not only enables us to examine
the variant impact of industrialization on traditional and contemporary patterns of work and employment but also highlights the
co-existence of complementary and conflicting types of formal and
informal economic practices. The literature on the major processes

affecting the structure of formal employment was utilized to illustrate the constantly shifting boundaries between work and employment and between the formal and informal economy. While a number of key trends were identified, the subsequent case studies examined revealed the importance of local, regional and national factors on seemingly universal trends. Differences in the structure of the formal and informal economy between different countries is often acknowledged in the literature but less attention is generally given to local and regional variations within specific countries. Yet a comparison of the significance of the informal economy within and between countries such as Italy, Spain and Greece reveals the crucial role that local political alliances play in developing lucrative or exploitative aspects of the informal economy. The general conclusion of the chapter is that flexible specialization encourages the growth and development of informal economic activities but the remainder of the book demonstrates the local, regional and national consequences of this trend. Often, mass production and flexible specialization are put forward as two contrasting alternatives. By contrast, the rest of the chapters illustrate how capitalism has always contained flexible and inflexible elements. Hence what we are witnessing are new shifts in each rather than a simple trend towards greater flexibility (Sayer, 1989).

4 Informal Employment in Europe and the United States

The previous chapter suggested that industrialization in Europe and the USA resulted in the adoption of the Fordist model of production and that this method of production gradually fell into disrepute during the economic crises of the 1970s and 1980s. Mass production in large scale enterprises gave way to flexible specialization and decentralization putting small scale industries at the centre of the industrial strategies of modern capitalist economies. Flexible specialization ironically arises as a direct result of the development of large scale production itself because large scale production requires increasing standardization which enhances the demand for niche products to cover markets which cannot be satisfied by the standardized product (Pederson *et al.* 1994). This is not to suggest that mass production and flexible specialization are mutually exclusive alternatives as both are likely to co-exist rather than outcompete each other (Sverrisson, 1994). However, the trend towards flexible specialization is likely to create informal employment opportunities for people who are often peripheral within the mainstream labour market.

Enterprises venturing into smaller more unstable markets often rely on unskilled labour which can be hired or fired at short notice. This enables the enterprise to respond to uncertainty and instability in the market. Larger firms decentralize through the use of subcontracting and often rely on sweatshops and small scale artisan-type enterprises to enable them to cope with fluctuations in the volume of differentiated consumer demand. Instability in the economy forces certain groups of people to rely for their survival on a complementary mix of formal and informal wage labour and in some cases this is supplemented by inadequate and often sporadic welfare provision which in turn enhances incentives to become involved in wage labour in informal ways. Hence, people's association with the formal labour market becomes increasingly blurred as they are often forced into increasingly precarious informal ways of making a living.

The chapter examines these trends by focusing on how vulnerable groups in the formal labour market become attractive as expendable employees for enterprises seeking to achieve flexibility. While informality does not necessarily reside in the characteristics of the workers, nonetheless a focus on the participants in informal economic activity may tell us a great deal about the workings of the informal economy. Informal economic activity often intensifies the segmentation of the labour market along age, gender, class and ethnic lines. The experiences of women are dealt with separately in Chapter 6. Here, the emphasis is on the unemployed, ethnic minorities, children and moonlighters. This is not meant to be an exhaustive account of all the participants in informal employment. Rather these groups most effectively illustrate how the precarious and changing nature of formal employment leads to the adoption of informal employment strategies among employers and groups of individuals most effected by the decline in formal job opportunities.

There are of course notable absences here. The old aged for example may continue to contribute to the workings of the economy by engaging in sporadic, informal employment. Their motivations may stem from economic necessity as they may not receive any state allowances while others may find that the allowances that they receive from the relevant authorities are insufficient to meet their basic needs or to meet the standard of living to which they have become accustomed. Others may engage in non-standard types of employment through a need to ensure that they continue to play a useful economic role in society at large. The need or desire of the old aged to engage in a few hours employment per week may suit employers who require an informal, flexible, part-time workforce.

Students may provide further recruits for employers seeking flexibility in employment conditions. Rising participation in university education in most advanced industrial countries has resulted in large numbers of students seeking temporary or vacational employment to help meet their material needs. The rising cost of education encourages students to find some type of part-time employment, either formal or informal, to support themselves or help alleviate the support given by their families for their higher education. Students may become involved in occupations appropriate to their final destinations and hence achieve valuable experience at a low cost to the employer who may gain high quality labour at marginal cost. On the other hand, students may be found working in a range of mainly service or labour intensive occupations such as bars, cafes, restaurants, night clubs and so on. Students are often in competition with other marginal workers for these types of low-grade jobs such as the unemployed, immigrant workers, married women seeking part-time employment and multiple job holders. However, the fact that students often regard this labour as temporary may make them more willing employees and less susceptible to the discontent induced by the lack of alternatives experienced by these other groups.

The self-employed are also likely to play a substantial role in the informal economies of most European countries and the US. Indeed some commentators regard the informal economy as simply tax evasion by the self employed. Self employed individuals and owners of small businesses may seek ways of avoiding tax payments to the state. In countries such as the UK, where tax is deducted at source from employees' salaries, self employment provides the most viable way of evading tax. Pahl (1990) argues that the informal economy in the UK is almost entirely a problem of tax evasion by those in self-employment. They may do this through under-declaring levels of profit and income and inflating expenses. The self employed may also informally employ other people off-the-books and pay them in cash. They may also use the unpaid labour of family members. For example, small scale owners of shops and restaurants in Greece often rely on the unpaid labour of wives and children making it difficult to accurately categorize women and children's economic input. The agricultural sector also depends heavily on the unpaid work of women and children. A certain amount of this often invisible labour is statistically visible under the classification 'assisting and non-paid family members'. Hadjimichalis and Vaiou (1988) estimate that as much as one third of the female population in employment in Greece is classified as 'assisting and non-paid family members'. In instances like these, employer relations become confused with family relations as employers are also husbands and fathers.

The four types of informal employment covered in this chapter demonstrate the heterogeneity of informal employment. Each of the examples overlap as they are all aimed at defrauding the tax or welfare benefit system either by informal wage labourers themselves or those who employ informal wage labourers. As labour becomes more expensive due to taxes and welfare contributions, informal employment becomes increasingly attractive and competitive. Employers may seek to escape the rigidity of the institutional conditions of employment by seeking flexible forms of informal wage labour. For example collective bargaining agreements have severely restricted the availability of workers for overtime or made overtime too expensive for many employers. An informal flexible supply of labour may enable employers to fulfil their additional needs without meeting the demands of collective bargaining agreements. The more heterogeneous and fragmented employment becomes, the more regulatory systems will find it harder to cope and the more opportunities will thus arise for informal employment practices to emerge.

Of course, flexible employment practices do not just take place in the informal economy. As the previous chapter indicated, the UK economy has been characterized by legalized de-regulation for the past decade. Indeed the UK has one of the highest ratios of part-time to full-time employment in Europe and the number of temporary, casual, non-standard forms of employment continues to grow. Because of a lack of any great restraints on employers of formal labour, very little of the flexible employment practices that characterized the UK economy take place informally. Hence in relation to Europe as a whole, the informal economy in the UK is likely to be small (Pahl, 1990). Nonetheless, the UK is not immune from the post-Fordist strategies of flexible specialization and the growth in subcontracting within the UK is likely to produce increasingly diverse patterns of formal and informal employment.

Let us now turn to an examination of moonlighters, the unemployed, immigrants and children in order to illustrate some of the above trends. These groups are often in competition with each other for the low-paid, temporary, informal employment opportunities that are becoming increasingly available.

MULTIPLE JOB HOLDERS AND MOONLIGHTERS

Moonlighters, like multiple job holders, have access to more than one job. These people often transmit the boundaries of the formal and informal economy by having an occupation in the formal economy and an additional undeclared job in the informal economy. These activities are not inherently illegal or informal. For example, a person may obtain their livelihood through an amalgamation of a number of part-time jobs all of which are declared to the relevant authorities. Another person may have an additional job to their formal full-time occupation but may declare their additional income to the appropriate inland revenue department. Indeed, some European countries and the United States are quite efficient at monitoring tax payers and have developed statistical measures of participation in double-job holding. In Italy, for example, ISTAT produces official estimates of multiple job holding. However, these statistics are obviously limited to those who declare their multiple activities for tax purposes. The statistics tend to relate to cases where there is an accumulation of part-time jobs and where no one occupation is dominant. It also includes cases where tax demands would be negligible and where there would be little incentive for the participant to conceal the activity. This would apply to those who earn a limited amount of officially declared income on top of their full-time earnings.

Multiple job holding is widespread among farmers in a number of European countries. The decline in agricultural income and underemployment of agricultural workers have forced many to seek additional part-time work. In Southern Italy, Spain, Portugal, Ireland, France and Greece, agricultural workers and farmers have had to look for other complementary part-time work and in many cases such work has been an irregular but necessary supplement to the income gained from farming. (see Final Synthesis Report on the Underground Economy published by the Commission of the European Communities). Take, for example, Damianos *et al.*'s (1992) account of the trend towards multiple job holding among farmers in Greece. Over a quarter of the Greek labour force is employed in agriculture. However, small, fragmented land-holdings, insufficient and poorly organized marketing of agricultural produce and low levels of rural infrastructure mean that many farmers have to engage in additional employment activities in order to make ends meet. The development of tourism and housing construction in rural Greece, together with state incentives from the mid 1970s onwards to curb internal migration by decentralizing investment to the less developed regions of the country, provide farmers with opportunities to engage in multiple job holding.

Drawing on national empirical evidence and surveys, Damianos *et al.* (1992) outline the impact multiple job holding has on different types of farming households in Greece. They refer to the first type of household as 'non-agricultural'. This term is applied to small farms of less than one hectare where family needs are met largely by wage labour outside the farm in industry, tourism and construction. The second type refers to 'worker-peasant' households. These households increasingly resort to multiple job holding due to continuous structural changes in agriculture. Farms here are around three hectares but do not provide the necessary resources to fulfil family needs leaving male farmers with little option but to engage in permanent multiple job holding. The third type identified by Damianos *et al.* refers to 'farm households'. Here holding areas are above average and farm work remains the main source of income. However, farming viability depends on modernization and expansion and involvement in multiple job holding is based on meeting these objectives. Damianos *et al.* refer to a fourth less numerically significant type of household which they term 'farm business households' where multiple job holding is solely connected to agriculture concerned with expanding agricultural activities in trading and processing agricultural produce. While involvement of the first three households in multiple job holding is motivated by necessity rather than choice, in this latter category, farmers choose to become involved in multiple job holding in order to further develop their farming businesses. As can be seen from this case study, multiple job holding may have different local and regional effects in specific countries apart from national differences between countries.

While moonlighting and multiple job holding is not necessarily an invisible form of employment, Mingione (1990a:41–2) suggests that in relation to Italy, three factors may promote the non-reporting of additional income. Firstly, tax on personal income is levied at a highly progressive rate. This means that the tax levied on additional income is likely to be very high making concealment an attractive option. Secondly, the Italian fiscal system is highly inefficient at tracing income from irregular employment, hence the risk of detection is very low. Finally, tax deductions for family needs are low. This means that married people end up paying the same tax as single people and may attempt to ease this burden and fulfil family needs by engaging in additional undeclared economic activity. A similar situation exists in Greece where the typical moonlighter is likely to be a married man with a family to keep. As in Italy, married men are treated no differently from single men in terms of preferential tax and welfare entitlements, hence many need an additional job to fulfil family needs. Vinay (1985) suggests that the incentive to undertake more than one job increases in households where there is more than one pre-school age child. This is because the presence of pre-school age children reduces the involvement of women in market activities making it necessary for the male to take on a second job in order to meet family needs. A survey carried out in 1977 in the United States (DeGrazia 1984) found that one in three of the almost five million moonlighters surveyed stated they were compelled to take a second job to meet everyday family expenses.

Increases in tax burdens, cutbacks in welfare benefit entitlements coupled with state policies to curb inflation and deal with the worldwide recession may force specific family members into holding more than one occupation. While in some cases this may enable households to continue to fulfil their basic needs, in other cases, the motivation may come from a desire to maintain a high standard of living (Alden 1981; Stinson, 1990). Accountants and teachers for example, may take on extra work on the side in order to maintain or improve their social status. This is likely to be the case in peripheral countries in Europe where the introduction of austerity measures may result in a fall in real income. Moreover, those involved in the production of services may find it easier to engage in additional work as the exchange of services is likely to be much less regulated than the exchange of goods.

Workers in the United States and most European countries tend to work less hours per week than at the turn of the century and this 'frees' many to take up additional work if they so desire. In Italy, Greece, Spain and Portugal, civil servants, teachers and bank clerks who finish work in the early afternoon find themselves in a favourable position to take on additional work related to their primary occupation. Teachers account for more than a quarter of all moonlighters in Italy (Mingione, 1990a). Similarly in the US, as many as 20 per cent of teachers hold second jobs (Bell and Roach, 1989). These jobs do not refer to occupations undertaken during vacation periods but to concurrent jobs held by teachers which often extended their working week to 70 or 80 hours. Mingione (1990a) found that the 'typical' moonlighter in Italy increases his annual number of working hours by approximately one third. Pahl's (1984) research in the UK revealed similar findings relating to tradesmen such as builders, car mechanics, electricians and plumbers. These tradesmen often undertook extra sporadic work in the evenings and did not declare their additional earnings to the relevant tax authorities. Shift workers also provide ideal recruits for second job holding. In a study of firemen in the UK, Edgell and Hart (1988) found that 60 per cent of those interviewed worked informally as well. The occupational regulations relating to firefighting do not allow firefighters to hold second jobs, hence additional jobs must be concealed. The majority of firemen interviewed by Edgell and Hart did not declare their additional earnings.

DeGrazia (1984) argues that traditionally moonlighting and multiple job holding were restricted to a few economic sectors such as agriculture and construction work or were the preserve of specific categories of workers such as teachers, firemen and policemen. However, evidence from Europe and the US indicates that these practices are becoming more widespread and affecting a greater variety of economic sectors and a larger number of both manual and non-manual workers. Eyler (1989) found that in an era of corporate downsizing and transnational capital flight, some white collar and management workers in the US turn to moonlighting as a way of experimenting with second careers or acquiring new skills and contacts in case these were needed due to the possibility of losing their full-time jobs. Skolka (1987:41) argues that in France, moonlighting is common in construction, clothing, mechanics, industrial design, leather products, book-keeping, hairdressing, agriculture and in seasonal occupations. Bawly (1982) found a similar diversity of occupations among second job holders in the US. Waldinger (1992) found that hotels in Philadelphia and New York rely on middle-class actors for whom working in hotels is secondary to meet labour requirements that reflect the class characteristics of guests. In this way, hotels are able to secure flexibility at low cost.

It is clear then that moonlighting covers a heterogeneous group of people. Despite common notions that moonlighters work because they are financially deprived (Jamal, 1986), it is obvious that relatively well paid workers also engage in moonlighting and that on occasions moonlighting may prepare workers for new careers. On the other hand, the availability of workers willing to engage in moonlighting is very beneficial to employers seeking to gain flexibility in working arrangements. The ability of workers to find more than one job perpetuates the trend towards part-time, sporadic, unstable jobs as many workers are not totally dependent on income from one source. Low-wage rates can also be compensated for by obtaining additional employment. In many countries, collective bargaining agreements have severely restricted the use of overtime or made overtime too expensive for many employers to afford. Moonlighting can enable employers to maintain competitiveness and achieve flexibility in an increasingly uncertain economic environment. By paying lower hourly wage levels, avoiding tax and social security contributions and other legal restrictions governing formal labour, employers can gain access to a flexible workforce through moonlighting.

Chronaki *et al.* (1993), for example, argue that diffused industrialization in Greece depends to a large extent on a workforce that is available at any moment and compelled to accept unfavourable working conditions. The irregularity of employment and subsequently income in the overall economy obliges workers to seek second or third jobs to cover slump periods and to mobilize the whole family to fulfil orders during peak periods. Mingione (1990a) argues that the industries affected by decentralization are the most likely to make use of moonlighters. To Mingione, moonlighting plays an essential role in making it possible for small enterprises linked to the process of decentralization to secure a high degree of flexibility at a low cost. Moonlighters themselves exploit the flexibility in working hours attached to their main job and their involvement in moonlighting often leads to 'controlled absenteeism' (1990a:6). Hence, the practice of multiple job holding enables employers and moonlighters to maintain flexibility and respond to fluctuating demands for labour.

UNEMPLOYMENT AND THE INFORMAL ECONOMY

Since the economic recession which has plagued western industrial states since the 1970s, there has been a rapid increase in unemployment levels in European countries and in the United States of America. Unemployment is a permanent state of affairs for an increasing number of people throughout the 'developed' world. Given this expansion in unemployment and cutbacks in welfare benefits and entitlements which have characterized advanced economies since the 1970s, it seems likely to assume that the unemployed would provide ideal recruits for informal employment opportunities as and when such opportunities become available. In a study carried out for the International Labour Office (ILO) in 1984, DeGrazia suggested that a substantial proportion of the unemployed were involved in the 'black economy'. She quotes studies estimating the numbers of 'working unemployed' as 50 per cent of unemployed workers in the Seville area of Spain, 15 per cent of the unemployed in the US, 27.8 per cent of the unemployed in Italy and estimates ranging from 40 per cent to 80 per cent in France (DeGrazia, 1984:17). However, these high estimates have been undermined by a spate of studies throughout the 1980s and 1990s which indicate that the unemployed are the least likely group to participate in the informal economy in Europe and the US.

DeGrazia relied on a combination of academic and media reports for her statistics on the numbers of 'working unemployed'. Media reports are notoriously unreliable as indicators of the existence of social security abuse. Often, such reports highlight a few spectacular examples and these are mistakenly utilized to imply a common trend. Wenig (1990b) suggests that such reports often receive a disproportionate degree of public attention and this says more about political values and the role of the mass media than it does about unemployed people themselves. Pahl (1990) argues that despite the increasing number of studies which confirm the quantitative unimportance of the unemployed in informal paid employment, the issue continues to receive a disproportionate degree of media and government attention centering on the undeserving poor and reaffirming the moral values surrounding formal employment.

The fact that a small percentage of the unemployed does find informal employment opportunities is utilized to indicate that the economy is more buoyant than high levels of unemployment indicate and these trivial instances justify policies which invest considerable resources in uncovering possible benefit fraud. Since the unemployed are often considered to be not dependent on welfare benefits alone, this creates a climate of opinion in which unemployment is explained primarily in terms of the attitudes and behaviour of the unemployed rather than by a downturn in the economy lowering the demand for labour (Hakim, 1992). Moreover, since some states are facilitating the creation of badly paid, exploitative formal jobs, then unemployment must continue to be seen as an unpleasant experience to be avoided at all costs. Hence, some states adopt contradictory policies of severely penalizing the small numbers of unemployed who are caught working while introducing policies to restrict benefits to those who can prove that they are actively seeking work.

As formal job opportunities become scarcer and since much of the employment that is available is so badly paid and insecure then some individuals may indeed be motivated to seek informal employment. However, those with strong incentives to work informally may find they have relatively few opportunities to do so. There is a general consensus among researchers into informal economic activity in most European countries and North American states that the unemployed are unlikely to participate in the informal economy. This is because of a variety of factors including the level of opportunities available, the extent to which informal employment is monitored by the state and other official agencies, the penalties for engaging in informal employment while officially classified as unemployed and the level and extent of welfare provision in different countries. These factors individually or collectively influence the level of participation by the unemployed in informal employment. Hence, while in general terms, the unemployed may be less likely to engage in informal employment compared to other groups, this rate may differ depending on the combination of the above factors in different nation states.

This section draws on a number of studies concerning the participation of the unemployed in informal employment. However, this aspect of the informal economy is notoriously difficult to research given the moral indignation which often surrounds this issue. Mattera (1985) suggests that given the periodic campaigns against supposed abuses of the welfare benefit systems in countries such as the UK and the US, it is very unlikely that people receiving these benefits will declare their involvement in informal employment regardless of the confidentiality assured in surveys into the nature of this phenomenon. While the section will draw on specific case studies which will demonstrate different rates of participation in informal employment among the unemployed, the general concurrence among these studies is that the unemployed are less likely than the employed to engage in informal employment due to lack of skills, transport and capital and lack of opportunities due to the probability of living in poor localities where employment opportunities either formal or informal are likely to be minimal (Pahl, 1984; Glatzner and Berger, 1988, Windebank, 1991).

A report carried out by the European Commission in 1991 indicated that the unemployed are liable to participate in some forms of informal employment where unemployment benefits or other social security transfers are low or unavailable and where many of those actually unemployed may not be registered. In countries where the unemployed receive low or no unemployment benefits, there are obviously considerable incentives for the unemployed to engage in informal employment when and where they can find the opportunity to do so. Often the jobs available are low-paid, irregular and highly exploitative. However, in the absence of adequate welfare provision, such jobs may provide individuals with a vital source of income essential to get by. States may recognize the ineffectiveness of their own welfare systems and, as in some Southern European countries, tacitly encourage involvement in paid work outside of formal employment. In these instances, the numbers engaged in informal employment may be difficult to calculate.

Lobo (1990a) reports on an interesting study carried out in the Andalucia and Catalognia regions of Spain which compared the participation of the unemployed in informal employment between those entitled to welfare benefits and those who received no welfare benefits. Overall about 30 per cent of those officially unemployed had access to some form of paid informal employment. However, significant differences emerged in the participation rate of those eligible for unemployment benefits. Among this group, only 12 per cent were willing to engaged in the unstable forms of paid employment available.

The unwillingness of the unemployed to become involved in informal employment is likely to be greater in countries where the penalties for earning money while drawing benefits are severe and where the system is policed so effectively that scope for involvement in informal employment is remote. Such attitudes are likely to be more acute within states with strong welfare provision. In (West) Germany, Wenig (1990a) argues that employment is held in very high esteem and success is defined in terms of having a formal paid occupation. Those with formal jobs are considered as contributing to the overall good of society while those without formal jobs are regarded as useless and partly to blame for their own situation. While the unemployed could regain some measure of self-worth through informal paid employment, efficient and inflexible control of the potential economic activities of the unemployed make this an unlikely practice. The unemployed are continually regarded with suspicion by the officially employed and any indication that the unemployed may indeed be working is liable to be reported to the relevant authorities. Research in other European countries (Pahl, 1984; Howe, 1990) has confirmed the suspicion surrounding the daily activities of the unemployed making participation in informal paid employment a slim possibility. This can also be illustrated by examining how tax evasion is handled within many countries compared to welfare benefit abuse. The latter is generally treated as much more morally unacceptable than the former and dealt with much more harshly (Cook, 1989).

Within (West) Germany the level of unemployment benefit is much higher than the rate in many other European states. This reduces the incentive of the unemployed to bolster their income with undeclared informal employment. Non-declaration of additional income is dealt with severely in (West) Germany and often carries a prison sentence. In other Northern European countries where such activities are effectively policed and where the penalties for earning money while claiming benefits are severe, the participation of the unemployed in informal employment remains low. While the moonlighters and multiple job holders described earlier may lose their additional income if caught, the unemployed may have their full entitlement to benefits removed and this possibility may act as a powerful disincentive against engaging in informal employment particularly since much of this activity is likely to be irregular and insecure for exploitative rates of pay.

It is clear then that the extent to which states attempt to enforce their own regulations has an impact on the involvement of the unemployed in sporadic paid informal employment. Where states such as (West) Germany and the US adopt policies of closely monitoring labour markets and punishing those who engage in benefit fraud, participation is likely to remain low. Where states such as Italy and Greece ignore such practices unless they exceed broad limits then participation is likely to be much higher. While states such as France and the UK which adopt an in-between position of strictly controlling benefit fraud while simultaneously pursuing deregulation policies may on the one hand curtail incentives to engage in informal employment and on the other hand increase the opportunities for such practices to emerge (Wenig, 1990b).

Of course up to now we have focused on individual motives for engaging in informal paid employment and their links to welfare and monitoring systems in different nation states. Opportunities to work informally may be promoted by firms seeking to obtain more flexibility in their labour requirements to enable them to remain competitive in an increasingly unstable economic environment. The existence of large numbers of unemployed workers who receive little or no welfare payments has encouraged the growth of a very flexible proportion of the labour force who can be brought in at regular intervals to meet the fluctuating needs of certain industries. The

construction industry is a classic example of this trend. The existence of a casual labour force in construction provides essential
support for many concerns which could not continue if they were
obliged to provide regular all year round employment for all their
workers. In Italy, ISTAT estimates that there are approximately
half a million irregular workers in the construction industry with
about 90 per cent working on building sites in the Southern regions. These workers have little opportunity to escape a lifetime of
poverty and marginalization. Periods of irregular, low-paid informal employment are combined with periods of inactivity funded by
welfare benefit entitlements. In some cases, workers are employed
formally for a number of weeks in order to qualify for welfare benefits
and then dismissed and re-instated as informal paid employees or
in winter months or periods of low demand left to manage solely
on welfare benefits.

This trend is also prevalent in Greece. In both countries, construction workers receive higher levels of unemployment benefit
partly due to the existence of powerful construction unions. This
benefit is conditional on a minimum number of weeks spent in
formal employment where contributions are collected from employers
and workers. Many firms officially employ workers for this minimum period and then either suspend their employment altogether
or bring the previously formally employed workers into the workforce
on an informal basis. While this practice is detrimental to the social security systems in both countries, it is very beneficial to employers and to a lesser extent employees who can more readily
cope with the flexible labour demands resulting from the sporadic
nature of their work (Mingione, 1990a,b).

These case studies indicate the presence of significant local and
regional variations. The existence of high numbers of unemployed
workers who do not receive benefits or receive inadequate benefits
has encouraged the development of a very flexible segment of the
labour force which can easily be used for irregular, casual work.
Edin (1991) argues that the rationale for state legislators in the
US to let benefit levels fall far behind inflation means that benefit
entitlements are often too low to live on and thus have to be supplemented by recipients working informally as well. Her research
documents how welfare recipients in Chicago conceal the income
made from informal employment because if they declared their
earnings, their welfare payments would be reduced by almost the
full amount of their earnings leaving them as poor as before. Lobo

(1990a) outlines a number of studies carried out in the Andalusia and Catalognia regions of Spain which indicate that 30 per cent of those officially unemployed do in fact work. However, the type of employment gained was irregular, low-paid and unstable.

These locality variations can also be demonstrated by considering the involvement of the unemployed in the informal economy in the UK. A number of studies (Pahl, 1984; Morris, 1987; Bradshaw and Holmes, 1989) have indicated that those in formal employment were more likely to have access to informal job opportunities as well. This was mainly due to the fact that while the unemployed had time on their hands, they did not have the money to buy the tools and resources necessary to engage in informal employment. They also had little access to information about informal job opportunities and their low level of skills also acted as a barrier to obtaining informal employment. However, a number of other studies have revealed much higher levels of participation in the informal economy by the unemployed. Jordan (1992) found that two thirds of their sample of poor households had access to paid informal employment which they did not declare to the relevant authorities. MacDonald's (1994) research in Cleveland found that working while claiming benefits was a way of life and justified by informants as a necessary strategy in order to make ends meet.

Informal employment opportunities stemmed from subcontractors who often paid low wages for work that was often irregular rather than stable. In these circumstances, MacDonald argues it made little sense for claimants to sign off welfare, lose their benefits and then be faced with the slow bureaucratic procedure of reapplying for welfare benefit. MacDonald argues that the availability of the unemployed willing to work for low wages, for short intensive periods, enabled subcontractors in particular to gain greater flexibility from workers. Subcontractors hoping to secure tenders offered informal employment to people they knew were in receipt of welfare benefits and were therefore able to 'afford' to work for very low rates of pay.

Similar observations were evident from the hiring procedures of small-scale subcontractors in the construction industry in Belfast (Leonard, 1994). According to Mattera (1985), throughout western European industry there has been a substantial increase in the amount of work going to subcontractors. Subcontracting describes a system whereby the overall employer pays for an agreed period of labour time but leaves the organization, manning and sometimes the equipping of the task to the subcontractor. Main employers gain considerable benefits from employing subcontractors. Firstly, subcontracting offers the main employer a relatively inexpensive means of determining the price for a definable area of work because rates for particular operations are widely recognized and in depressed conditions, strong competition between subcontractors for work will tend to lower the general level of prices. Secondly, subcontracting enhances employers' flexibility in dealing with fluctuating product markets. In the case of construction work, subcontracting enables employers to cope with the seasonal fluctuations associated with the industry. The main employer can call in or lay off labour when needed and this in turn reduces fixed costs. Thirdly, by employing subcontractors on short-term contracts, much labour legislation can be avoided. Finally, the low level of trade unionization among subcontract workers enhances control over the labour process (Bresnen, 1985).

Subcontracting plays a major role in capital's new emphasis on flexibility in working practices. Callaghan (1986) argues that subcontracting enables employers to create or strengthen the development of two-tier employment. This involves the insulation of a central core of workers (deemed to be the most important to the firm's operation) from the wider labour market and another tier of workers who are not on standard employment contracts and who often experience inferior pay and job security. The use of a flexible, non-unionized labour force is often a necessary condition for survival in the cut-throat competition among subcontractors (Mattera, 1985). Employing labour off-the-books is one of the most effective means of keeping costs low. In Belfast, attempts to do this are facilitated by the large number of unemployed men with wives who are also excluded from the formal labour market.

Small-scale subcontractors dominate the construction industry in Belfast. They generally work on short-term contracts carrying out household construction, repairs and renovations. In some cases, they carry out work once done by public housing bodies. The policy to privatize public industries and services further enhances job opportunities for small-scale construction subcontractors. These subcontractors generally secure contracts through the competitive tendering process whereby the cheapest tender often secures the contract. One of the main ways of cutting costs is to reduce labour costs and subcontractors do this by employing a mixture of formal and informal employees. Since the informal employees also claim welfare benefits, this justifies the paying of very low wages to these employees. These wages are supplements rather than replacements for inadequate welfare benefits. Neither income is sufficient on its own and it is only through an amalgamation of both sources of income that households are able to secure a reasonable standard of living. The practice of working while claiming benefits has become so prevalent in some areas that standard informal wage rates are in operation whereby subcontractors calculate different rates for skilled, semi-skilled and unskilled workers on the basis of benefits plus wages (Leonard, 1994). Wives of unemployed men were also employed by contract cleaning firms on a similar basis (Leonard, 1992).

This case study indicates some of ways in which opportunities for informal employment are connected to the development of flexibility in working practices. It also indicates the importance of locality and regional differences in facilitating or restricting the access of the unemployed to informal employment opportunities. Because of the nature of the political situation in Northern Ireland, the detection of welfare benefits abusers is more difficult and dangerous. Local cultural attitudes justify working while claiming benefits as an acceptable way of life because the depressed state of the local economy makes declared work more difficult to obtain.

Of course, it is difficult to generalize from specific case studies. The overwhelming evidence indicates that the unemployed have restricted access to informal employment opportunities. Even in Belfast, such work practices were often trivial in terms of the money earned and job vacancies were, sporadic and precarious. Informal employment rarely provided participants with viable alternatives to formal, secure, full-time employment but rather functioned as necessary additions to insufficient welfare entitlements. Moreover, opportunities to engage in informal employment were extremely limited and linked to informal information networks. Hence, this type of informal employment was characterized by numerous internal inequalities.

While the statistical significance of the involvement of the unemployed in informal employment remains weak, nonetheless, it is important not to ignore local and regional variations. To do so is to disregard the conditions which give rise to this type of informal practice. The fact that earnings from this type of informal economic activity are marginal and need to be supplemented by welfare benefits or by other formal or informal economic strategies only further reiterates the links between the formal and informal economy.

IMMIGRANTS AND THE INFORMAL ECONOMY

Contemporary national and international migration may also tell us a great deal about the changing nature of work. According to Miles (1990), migration is a structural feature of the capitalist mode of production in that those who sell their labour power as a means of economic survival are encouraged to move from one spatial location to another in response to the ever changing demands of capital for labour. This economic determinant of migration equally explains the movement of people within and across national boundaries although in the case of international migration, the nation state in policing its spatial and cultural borders, plays a mediating factor in the process of migration. This leads Miles to suggest that the rise of the nation state as a political unit is a crucial factor in the relationship between capitalist development and migration. Drawing on the work of Marx and Weber, Miles argues that both suggested that the prior formation of a strong state capable of exercizing political domination within a specific territory was a necessary precondition for the emergence of the capitalist mode of production. The emergent capitalist class prospered within specific spatial and political units. Hence the expansion of the capitalist mode of production occurred simultaneously with the spatial division of the world into nation states.

This focus on the nation state as a mediating factor in encouraging and discouraging migration enables analyses of migration to move beyond simplistic accounts which concentrate exclusively on capitalism as a unidimensional, all pervasive system. The state possesses the necessary powers to grant both the right of access and withdrawal from one national boundary to another. While Miles recognizes that the ever changing demand for labour arising from the capitalist accumulation process is a major reason for migration within and into capitalist societies, nonetheless he emphasizes the role of the nation and state in mediating the labour demand and supply factors that influence international migrations. It follows from this analysis that the state may play a major role in influencing the amount of labour power available for work in the informal economy. By denying some people formal, legal access to their territorial boundaries, the state leaves some migrants with little option but to become involved in informal economic strategies as a means of economic survival.

This section examines the role of migrant labour in the informal economies of Europe and the United States. The focus is primarily on male migrant workers. The incorporation of migrant women into the informal economy is assessed in Chapter 6. The discussion here focuses mainly on unskilled, unqualified migrants at the lower end of the labour market. This is not to deny the migration flows of professional and technical workers. Such flows have been increasing in importance in recent years particularly from the periphery to the centre of the world system. However, these workers possess skills which are in short supply in both the country of origin and migrant destination. Hence such workers are unlikely to end up in the informal economy. Moreover, the migration of highly skilled managerial, professional and technical workers is rarely defined as politically and ideologically problematic by the state. However, migrants destined for the lower end of the labour market have been variously welcomed as suppliers of scarce labour and rejected as responsible for rising unemployment among indigenous populations dependent on the way individual nation states have been affected by capitalist restructuring at specific points of time.

Analysis of post–1945 migration flows into Western Europe reveals the role of the state in initiating or sanctioning temporary migration in order to fulfil the ever changing demand for labour arising from the capital accumulation process. The post-war labour shortage in Europe meant that unskilled and semi-skilled labour had to found from somewhere and as cheaply as possible. Labour shortages were often met by migration into Europe from less economically and socially advanced regions both within and outside the European Community. Kofman and Sales (1992:31) suggest that three patterns were discernible in these post-war migration flows. The first pattern relates to colonial immigration where former colonial powers such as France and the UK recruited labour from their former colonies as part of the decolonization process. Black African immigrants came to be seen as a cheap labour source for French employers who employed them in unskilled and poorly paid jobs. Most workers entered France legally obtaining working permits from the French National Immigration Office although a significant number entered illegally and the Immigration Office generally legalized their status of guest worker after they had spent some time working in France (Barou, 1987). In Britain, immigrants from former colonies became Commonwealth citizens and acquired in theory rights as citizens in Britain. The second pattern concerns European powers such as Germany who obtained their labour power from peripheral areas of Europe. Immigrants were brought into Germany to fill specific gaps in the labour market usually low-status manual occupations that were unattractive to the indigenous population. They were generally recruited as guest workers or as temporary workers and were expected to leave after a fixed contract term (Yucel, 1987). The third pattern refers to post-war migration and relates to the relatively recent countries of immigration within Europe such as Spain, Italy and Portugal who attracted labour from the Southern Mediterranean and the Middle East. The fall of the Iron Curtain, ethno-political conflicts and civil and inter-state wars have created new refugee flows which have influenced migration patterns throughout the 1990s. This has led to a flow of migrants from Eastern Europe, Turkey, Algeria and the Balkans to Western Europe. The main destinations have been Germany, Sweden, Austria, Switzerland and Greece (Munz, 1996). While some of these migrants eventually obtain legal status, a number are destined for the irregular employment opportunities which characterize many western European countries.

UNDOCUMENTED MIGRANTS AND IRREGULAR EMPLOYMENT

The world-wide recession that hit Europe in the 1970s resulted in many European countries closing off their borders to new migration and adopting policies to repatriate existing migrants. Within this context, undocumented migration to European countries has increased, paving the way for the employment of these workers in less regulated informal sectors of the economy. Traditionally, migrants, whether or not they enter a country legally or illegally, represent a vulnerable, cheap and easily expendable workforce. Regardless of their prior skills they are often employed in poorly paid unskilled occupations not filled by the indigenous population. Lazaridis' (1996:344) interviews with Albanian migrant labourers in Greece indicate that highly skilled Albanian workers end up in low-skill, menial jobs. She quotes one respondent as saying 'I was working as an engineer in Albania . . . . . . now, I work as a gardener in the winter and I clean the beach in front of a luxury hotel in the summer'. While some migrants do manage to find permanent employment or achieve upward mobility through self-employment (see Saunders and Nee, 1996), others face a lifetime of poorly re- warded work. Where migrants enter a country illegally, they are likely to find it more difficult to find permanent, skilled employ- ment and become clandestine, undocumented labourers. The re- sort to illegal entry forcing immigrants into illegal work leads to the non-registration of school children and the non-use of social services in general. Buechler (1987) quotes studies in France and Germany that indicate up to one fifth of all foreign parents evade sending their children to school in order to remain undetected in the country. In these circumstances, disadvantages may be passed on to children who in turn will often experience the labour market in peripheral, informal ways.

Irregular migration may have a distorting effect on receiving labour markets because employers in certain sectors come to rely increas- ingly on sources of cheap, flexible, easily exploitable labour which are not available in the national labour supply (Collinson, 1993). Hence immigration does not necessarily displace indigenous work- ers as often the jobs available are ones rejected by the national workforce. Some entrepreneurs, particularly in labour intensive production sectors, may depend on irregular labour to remain in business. The availability of undocumented workers willing to work for low wages without adherence to welfare and employment legis- lation may permit small scale entrepreneurs to remain competitive and cope with fluctuations in the market. Romaniszyn (1996) found that the presence of undocumented Poles in Athens was very con- ducive for construction companies and for the families of middle- class professionals who were able to use a relatively unregulated labour system to lower their costs. Salt (1993) suggests that most new immigrants in southern Europe tend to be employed at the margins of the labour market or in parallel informal labour mar- kets which are largely uncontrolled and operate in the absence of collective bargaining systems. The mainly illegal immigrants found in these corresponding labour markets experience poor living and working conditions, have no union representation and no social security.

Lazaridis' (1996) research into Albanians in Greece provides an example of this trend. She estimates the number of illegal Alba- nian immigrants in Greece as 150 000 in 1993. Most enter the country with the assistance of highly developed smuggling networks. In general terms, Albanians have a standard of living below the poverty line.

They generally end up in low-skilled jobs which are unattractive to Greek workers. They provide employers with an extremely flexible, low-cost workforce. Lazaridis argues that employers do not need to replace labour with technology due to the existence of pools of easily exploited labour. These undocumented workers accept poor working conditions and work longer hours for lower wages than those offered to Greeks doing the same job. Sometimes their wages can be up to 50 per cent below those of Greek workers. Their illegal status places them in an extremely weak bargaining position and often they have little option but to accept the conditions established by their employers. Similarly, Leman's (1997) research into undocumented migrants in Brussels demonstrates that migrants are aware that their success in finding employment is largely due to the fact that they are willing to work at times of the day and night that native workers or legally resident migrants would not consider for the same salary. Hence the flexibility of undocumented migrants both contributes to their success in gaining employment and perpetuates the conditions which exploit their labour power.

Salt (1993) suggests that by the year 2000, approximately five million foreigners will be working throughout Europe and of this number only about two million are likely to be regularized migrants. Illegal immigrants usually end up in labour intensive industries with unsocial working conditions. The more an industry is unregulated for the indigenous workforce, the more likely it is to be open to the inflow of unregulated migrants. Salt suggests that in France, illegal immigrants are likely to work in manufacturing, in Italy, they are likely to be working as unskilled labourers and domestic workers while in Spain they are more likely to work as waiters and farm workers. In Great Britain, the employment pattern of migrants is more varied but also relatively disadvantageous. West Indian men tend to predominate in unskilled or semi-skilled transport or factory work, Chinese men run the family restaurant trade, Greek and Turkish Cypriot men work in services and manufacturing and Italians are mainly found in catering and small businesses (Buechler, 1987). Leman (1997) found that undocumented Asian migrants from Pakistan, India and China were often employed in the construction industry in Brussels. Undocumented Polish migrants also found employment in the construction industry. Hence illegal immigrants are generally found in jobs at the bottom end of the labour market.

During the 1980s and 1990s, many European states tried to curb the problem of illegal immigration by enforcing stricter control of employers who employ illegal immigrant workers. This involved raiding premises suspected of employing clandestine immigrant labour, raising fees for employing alien workers and introducing penalties for illegally employing immigrants (Lazaridis, 1996; Yucel, 1987). German law is very harsh on the employers of illegal foreigners if work conditions are more hazardous than the norm for German workers. This is in response to the recognition that illegal foreigners are likely to be in a desperate situation having no access to social security, hence they must be able to find employment regardless of working conditions. Since safety regulations are quite costly in Germany, employers can violate these regulations and evade taxes and social security contributions by employing illegal foreigners. However, detection is treated seriously with employers facing up to three years in prison or costly fines (Wenig, 1990a).

Many states have introduced legalization programmes for clandestine workers. However, from his research in France, Barou (1987) argues that many undocumented workers do not want to be legalized in case they risk losing their illegal jobs which often have not been declared. As long as illegal immigrants are willing to work for low wages with no access to employment protection, there will be a demand for illegal immigrant labour. In Greece, migrant workers without a permit are paid less than half the minimum wage paid to Greek workers doing equivalent work (Mingione, 1987). Unlike Spain and Italy, where in the mid 1980s attempts were made to change the status of illegal immigrants by legalization regulations, no such policies have so far been implemented in Greece (Lazaridis, 1996). This prevents illegal immigrants in Greece from gaining access to more desirable forms of labour. Illegal migrant workers are particularly appealing to employers connected with labour intensive industries. The availability of clandestine labour willing to work for below average wages allows employers to evade taxes, employment, health and safety regulations. Hence illegal immigrants provide a vital source of cheap labour and allow many small scale employers, particularly through subcontracting, to remain competitive and buoyant in an increasingly unstable economic environment. Let us now turn briefly to examine these trends within the context of the US immigrant labour market.

The level of net migration to the United States during the second half of the 1980s was greater than the total net immigration in all other countries of the world combined, reaching almost three million during the period 1985 to 1990 (Collinson, 1993:9). While the sheer scale of this migration separates the US from other European countries, nonetheless, Collinson argues that some general patterns link both regions. As in Europe, the US has introduced policies which greatly restrict legal and independent immigration. The types of worker migration that continue to persist relate to the legal movements of highly skilled professional workers and to the illegal and clandestine migration of unskilled workers. These illegal workers are usually located between the margins of the formal and informal economy.

Sassen (1991) points out that the growth of the informal economy in many American cities is often seen as the result of immigration from developing countries. Immigrant workers are viewed as bringing traditional patterns of work with them to their new destinations. Hence, immigrants promote and maintain backward attitudes to work and encourage the development of backward sectors of the economy. In other words, the supposed inherent characteristics of the immigrant workforce tends to promote the unfavourable conditions within which immigrants work. Sassen, by contrast, views these circumstances as part of the logic of advanced capitalism which involves a downgrading of the work practices associated with many sectors of advanced economies. She argues that the existence of immigrant labour willing to work at low cost facilitated but did not create the spread of the informal economy in many US states.

Castells and Portes (1989) argue that the spread of small-scale enterprises with less than ten employees since 1965 has enhanced opportunities for informal employment. They also suggest that there is a close association between the location of these small-scale enterprises and areas of high immigrant concentration particularly in cities such as New York, Miami and San Diego. Chavez (1992) describes the informal employment of undocumented Mexican immigrants in San Diego. Such jobs were typically low-paid, violated fair labour standards and offered poor working conditions. The undocumented Mexicans who ended up in these jobs were generally recent arrivals who lacked English language skills and had limited education. However, just under 10 per cent of these workers had been in the United States for ten years or more indicating the difficulties of breaking out of this secondary labour market.

Simcox (1997) argues that labour intensive industries such as apparel, footwear, construction, furniture and electronics faced with the increasing pressure of international competition are forced to cut their labour costs in order to survive. One way of cutting labour costs is through the employment of immigrants on an informal basis. Sassen-Koob (1989) examines the extent of informalization within these industries in New York. She suggests that the number of Hispanics involved in the construction industry increased significantly throughout the 1980s and much of the increase is related to the trend towards subcontracting in the construction industry. Work that used to be carried out by unionized construction workers is increasingly farmed out to small-scale subcontractors who often rely on a non-unionized, unregistered workforce. The apparel industry is similarly characterized by a significant increase in the numbers of subcontractors involved in the industry with much of the work being put out to sweatshops and homeworkers. The electronics industry revealed similar practices although here opportunities for immigrant businesses to develop existed. Portes (1995) argues that for some immigrants, the informal economy provides an avenue for rapid economic ascent. On the other hand, since many immigrant businesses serve low-income immigrant communities, often the opportunities to accumulate capital are extremely limited. Sassen-Koob (1989) links the development of the 'gypsy cab' industry in New York to the failures of the formal transport system to meet the needs of low income immigrant and minority neighbourhoods. However, she warns that while many informal economic activities of immigrants are geared towards meeting the needs of their own internal economies, nonetheless, of equal significance is the extent to which immigrant labour meets and satisfies demand from the larger economy.

Access to low wage immigrant workers enables firms in the formal economy to compete with low wage workers in other countries. This is particularly important for the apparel industry. Subcontracting is an essential part of this process as work becomes decentralized to sweatshops and immigrants' homes where labour violations are common and where the intensification of labour can be enhanced at low cost. This fulfils the need for small-scale local firms to compete with cheap imports. The expansion of a high income workforce goes hand in hand with the trend towards informalization as their needs are often satisfied due to the presence of a vast supply of low wage immigrant workers (Sassen, 1996:584). Hence, the increasing separation of New York's population into a high income and low income strata feeds and perpetuates the informalizaton of labour. High income gentrification creates a demand for goods and services that are not typically mass produced or sold through mass outlets. This facilitates the development of non-unionized, small-scale labour intensive industries and a concomitant growth in sweatshops and homeworking. These structural transformations in the larger economy encourage firms, producers, consumers and workers to seek and supply flexible work practices. While immigrants are often ideally placed to respond to these needs, they do not create these needs and on occasion can utilize these strategies to their own advantage (see for example, Stepick, 1989; Simcox, 1997).

CHILD EMPLOYMENT AND THE INFORMAL ECONOMY

The economic contribution of children to their families, their communities and to society in general is rarely acknowledged. Children in Europe and the US are often portrayed as economically dependent on others. Where such children engage in any form of paid employment, this is generally viewed as a harmless pastime. Yet the ideal of childhood as a period of innocence without economic responsibilities bears little relation to most of the world's children. Whether in the UK, the United States, western or southern Europe, children's employment is often an essential component of the economy. Yet children remain invisible workers whether or not they are legally employed. This is because children are seen as inherently unproductive and because much of their employment is so poorly rewarded, they are generally excluded from the accounting methodologies which define and measure formal economic activity. The invisibility of children's labour is even more pronounced when it takes place within the informal economy. This section reviews the nature and extent of children's informal employment in order to highlight the reality of many children's economic lives.

There is a common assumption that child labour is an antiquated relic of the pre-capitalist era that would gradually be eroded with the further development of capitalist relations of production. Yet even in the most advanced countries of the world, children continue to play a significant role in the economy, often performing jobs also undertaken by adults. Of course throughout the twentieth century, the state has played an important part in shaping children's economic activities. The banning of child labour which commenced in Britain in the latter part of the nineteenth century spread throughout Europe and the US resulting in children combining paid work with education in most advanced economies. Hence, children came to be identified with a particular form of employment, that is out-of-school employment taking place before or after school, at weekends or during school holidays. This type of employment is rarely defined as exploitative child labour but as healthy, invigorating pastimes which children can carry out for extra pocket money and in the process learn the values of economic independence. However, much of the reality of child employment is far removed from this simplistic image.

Children present employers with an extremely flexible workforce. They can be brought in and out of the labour market to suit employers' fluctuating needs. They rarely join trade unions (indeed most trade unions contain no provisions for workers under school leaving age), hence they represent an extremely passive workforce. Because of the temporary status of their labour force participation, they can be employed in menial, poorly paid jobs with inadequate working conditions and poor career prospects. Finally, since they represent a marginal workforce, they are often employed illegally rather than legally, thus even the limited labour laws associated with individual national economies are often flouted.

Defining a 'child' is no easy task as definitions tend to vary from one country to another. The most common method used is chronological age yet even here disparities exist across one society to another. Often leaving school signifies the transition from childhood to adulthood. Yet even here problems exist. The minimum school leaving age varies from 14 to 16 years of age in many European countries. Where the child transfers from leaving school into further or higher education rather than employment, childhood is prolonged. Where the school leaver is unable to find employment, he/she occupies some limbo state between childhood and adulthood. In some southern European countries, there is often a gap of one or two years between the end of compulsory schooling and the minimum legal working age. This is particularly the case in Greece and Portugal and often these children end up working in the informal economy. Organizations such as the International Labour Organization (ILO) or United Nations have faced enormous hurdles when attempting to draw up international recommendations to safeguard the rights of children in employment because the age categories they advocate conflict with nation states' interpretations of childhood. The ILO adopted a minimum age convention set at 15 years of age in 1973 but to date only 27 countries have ratified the convention. In 1989, the UN adopted the Convention on the Rights of the Child defining a child as someone under 18 years of age. While the British government is a signatory to the UN convention, it feels that no action is required to implement the UN recommendations as despite evidence to the contrary (Lavalette *et al.* 1995), its existing legislation already meets the UN requirements. The British government has also sought an opt out from a European Union Labour and Social Affairs directive (1993) intended to severely restrict the work opportunities available to school children on the basis that such employment opportunities concern 'light' tasks undertaken by children for extra pocket money.

Positive images of child employment as an effective initiation into the adult world of work and responsibility emerges most strongly in the American literature on children and employment. Evidence gathered by D'Amico (1984), Light *et al.* (1985), Greenberger and Steinberg (1986), Green (1990) and Bachman and Schulenberg (1993) indicate that child employment is a significant feature of the labour market in the US. While these studies are not strictly comparable because of the different methodologies and definitions of children and employment utilized, nonetheless they indicate that child employment is a typical experience for most of American school children. The beneficial aspects of child employment emerge in a number of these studies. Green (1990), for example, argues that child employment can facilitate the transition from school to work and provide an arena to gain the material rewards necessary to have an independent life and peers. However, Greenberger and Steinberg (1986) while outlining a number of positive consequences associated with out-of-school employment, posit an equal number of negative effects which in many cases counteract the advantages. They suggest that engaging in out-of-school employment can have a detrimental effect on children's schooling, make them more acceptable of 'unethical' work practices and that the money and social contacts made may open up access to 'deviant' pastimes such as drinking, smoking and taking drugs. An earlier study by Steinberg *et al.* (1981) also indicated that out-of-school employment may go against the aims of the 'work ethic' enshrined in modern capitalism. This is because children are likely to be engaged in menial types of employment and thus adopt a cynical attitude to work comprising of getting things done as quickly as possible with the minimal amount of effort.

Hence although out-of-school employment may have positive and beneficial effects for many children, for others, out-of-school employment may lead to exploitation with negative effects. Children are a particularly vulnerable section of the labour force and poverty and economic backwardness can often push children into inappropriate forms of out-of-school employment. They are often employed in small-scale, labour-intensive enterprises where because of their relative cheapness, they can help the employer to compete with larger and more efficient units of capital.

Van Herpen (1990) from a review of child employment in a number of European countries including the UK, Germany, Italy, Spain and Portugal, regards children as a cheap and silent workforce. His research suggests that children are most likely to be found in unskilled, underpaid, informal and unprotected employment. Regulation of pay, working hours, health and safety insurance, and social security protection are likely to be absent in many cases. Because of the informal nature of the job and the illegality of the employment status of many children, they can be hired and fired to suit the needs of the employer. Often when they reach the legal working age they become less attractive to employers and too expensive to employ and are often replaced with a new batch of younger workers.

Since certain forms of child employment are prohibited in many European countries and the US, this makes it difficult to obtain accurate information on the number of children in employment. The ILO estimates that 142 000 children are employed in Spain, 114 000 in Italy and between 90 000 and 200 000 in Portugal. Indeed, along with Greece, Portugal is estimated to have the highest rates of children in employment in Europe, so much so that child labour is considered a national problem. Williams (1992) found that children between the ages of six and 14 were employed in shoe, clothing, cork, ceramics and textile factories. They often worked 10 to 12 hours per day making schooling impossible. Children from poor families who cannot afford education are often taken out of school and sent to work. This practice is exasperated by the high levels of adult unemployment which makes the employment of children necessary for many households' economic survival. Van Herpen reports that often when adults are seeking employment, the employer will ask for the child of the applicant instead, resulting in the widespread employment of 10, 11 and 12 year old children receiving less than half the wage levels that would be paid to adults doing similar work.

In Greece, it is estimated that about 170 000 children between the ages of 12 and 18 are engaged in various forms of employment and only about 53 000 hold employment licences issued under the Ministry of Labour (Mingione, 1990c). This again means that the majority of children working in Greece are invisible workers. In the south of Italy, casual building workers often introduce their ten to 12 year old sons to casual building work. Sons help their fathers with illicit casual jobs and statistics on residential building in the south of Italy reveal large numbers of minors engaged in this work (Mingione, 1990b). Children often acquiesce with employers in their exploitation because they see their first introduction to the labour market as transitory and one that will pave the way for regular, guaranteed employment. However, often this is not the case. Instead some children transfer to a career of temporary employment. In the case of illicit construction work in Greece and southern Italy, once children reach the legal age of employment, they enter into competition with an abundance of available adult workers. As a result, many continue to learn the building trade through illicit casual work with few managing to become semi-skilled, regular employees.

Some estimates of the extent of children in employment in Italy place the figure as high as one and a half million (van Herpen, 1990). In the sweatshops of Naples and other regions of Southern Italy, the Italian trade union confederations estimate the numbers of children employed at around 100 000. In poor households, children's earnings from paid employment are essential to the family budget. Most children start work between the age of ten and 14 and as many as 45 per cent of all children do not finish their final year of primary schooling. Child employment predominates in the leather industry, glass-making, small-scale sweatshops and of course agriculture.

These case studies are backed up by a European report on child labour carried out in 1995 (CDEM, 1995). The report outlines the legislative framework affecting the employment of children in several European countries. While the legislation differs from one country to another, the report emphasizes that in most cases, the legislation covering the employment of children is inappropriate, out-of-date and poorly resourced. As a result, the way is paved open for the illegal employment of children in the informal economy. The report makes a distinction between positive and negative aspects of children's employment and uses the term 'child work' to refer to beneficial types of child employment and the term 'child labour' to refer to exploitative types of child employment. The report concludes that children throughout Europe are employed in situations which are not always beneficial to them but frequently harmful to their economic, social and educational development.

The overview of children's employment reviewed here presents a number of positive and negative examples of the uses of child labour in advanced industrial economies. The exploitation of children's labour power is likely to be worse in southern European countries where poverty and adult unemployment are more likely to restrict children's choice regarding the types of employment they may decide to engage in. In more affluent countries such as the US, France, Germany and the UK, children are likely to exercise more choice over their decisions to engage in out-of-school employment and participate in more beneficial types of work. White (1996) suggests that children living in more affluent circumstances are likely to be influenced by the globalization of consumer values and engage in out-of-school employment to keep up with the material possessions of their peers and advertising companies who actively and persistently target children as consumers. However, even within the most advanced capitalist economies, pockets of poverty persist and children living in inferior financial circumstances may be drawn into the labour market prematurely in highly exploitative ways. Some research indicates that child employment may reinforce gender and class inequalities and make it more difficult for children from unfavourable backgrounds to experience any form of upward social mobility (McKechnie *et al.* 1996, Leonard, forthcoming).

Finally, this focus on participation in out-of-school employment as an individual economic response on behalf of affluent or disadvantaged children and their families ignores the extent to which child employment forms a structural feature of the labour market in modern capitalist economies. The gradual removal of children from the general labour market throughout the twentieth century has facilitated their re-incorporation in more marginal ways. In many countries, child employment is combined with school attendance enhancing its invisibility and encouraging informal rather than formal uses of children's labour power. The trend towards flexibility means that many employers are able to reduce the number of regularly employed staff and employ two or three school pupils for one job, often in the absence of proper legal obligations on the part of the employer. The decentralization of production and the farming out of production tasks to artisan-type workshops and sweatshops encourages the further use of child labour. The growth in competition between American and European firms and competitors from less developed countries where child employment is more prevalent leads some unscrupulous employers in advanced economies to lower their labour costs through the employment of children. Children can be paid less than adult workers even when employed in the same jobs and tend to be more malleable and passive than adult employees. Interestingly, rates of child involvement in paid employment tend to be highest in areas with high rates of adult unemployment indicating that child workers may be used to undercut the employment of adults. Hence, rather than the twentieth century leading to the eradication of the employment of school children, the latter represent an increasingly marginalized yet crucial feature of the labour market in advanced capitalist economies.

THE 'HOUSEWIFIZATION' OF EMPLOYMENT

This chapter has provided a brief overview of some of the reasons why certain groups of workers become incorporated into the labour market in informal ways. Global economic restructuring has specific implications for the division of labour. While these implications will obviously have different effects in different places, nonetheless, they fuel a general trend towards the informalization of the economy. Flexible employment practices which are limited due to strong traditions of worker protection and regulation of employment conditions can be achieved through the creation of informal types of employment or through new types of non-standard formal employment. The specific forms these new working arrangements take will depend on complex negotiations between capital and labour and on whether the state facilitates or hinders the smooth running of the outcome of these negotiations. The era of full-time, long-term, stable male employment has been undermined by the development of less stable, less structured and more sporadic types of formal and informal employment. These new types of employment rely on a more diverse group of workers rather than the male 'breadwinner' model of employment. This model only applied to a limited range of countries for a limited period of time yet the model continues to act as a yardstick against which current forms of employment are assessed. Many workers are increasingly being brought into the labour market to undertake work that is temporary, part-time, unprotected, disorganized and without benefits, protection or state regulation. Mies (1986) refers to this development as 'housewifization'. This refers to a process whereby an increasingly wide range of workers find themselves in the situation of traditional housewives – disorganized, isolated and economically insecure. In this context, global restructuring is likely to have a salient influence in the lives of an increasingly heterogeneous group of people who despite different local, regional and national manifestations come to experience the labour market in increasingly similar ways.

5 Household Economic Strategies: Work Beyond Employment

The previous chapter focused on the responses of individuals to changes in the structure and organization of formal employment. As formal job opportunities become more fluid and unstable, some individuals attempt to maintain an acceptable standard of living by turning to informal employment practices. The chapter illustrated how the formally employed, the unemployed and different types of workers such as ethnic minorities and children fit in with capital's need for a flexible workforce. While a substantial proportion of the new flexible employment practices are available in the formal economy, others take place informally in order to escape regulation and detection. Economists and policy makers concerned with estimating the size and significance of the informal economy have been so preoccupied with these types of paid activities that they have often failed to acknowledge the additional unpaid work which individuals undertake in order to gain a level of economic security. Often these activities take place at the level of the household and have a profound influence on the involvement of individuals in both formal and informal paid employment. This chapter emphasizes the economic importance of the household in an age of economic uncertainty. Because the literature on household work strategies is immense, the discussion here is unavoidably selective, focusing on areas which best illustrate the workings of the informal economy. Hence, the main thrust of the chapter is on self provisioning within households and reciprocal transactions between households. These activities indicate the fallacy of focusing on the paid formal and informal employment practices of individuals without simultaneously considering the often complementary unpaid economic strategies of household members. It is only through an examination of the total economic activities of households, both paid and unpaid, that a comprehensive understanding of the connections between the formal and informal economy can be achieved.

HOUSEHOLDS AS UNITS OF PRODUCTION AND CONSUMPTION

Throughout the twentieth century, the household gradually lost its role as a unit of production and became increasingly important as a unit of consumption. This new role for the household was essential for Fordism to offload the fruits of its mass consumption techniques. The spread of consumerism encouraged household members to move towards the realm of formal paid employment in order to afford the goods that modern capitalism increasingly produced. Some commentators (Silver, 1996) even regard women's movement into paid formal employment as part of this process. By boosting the income of the household, more consumer durables could be purchased. According to this view, time becomes a scarcer commodity for employed housewives leading to an increased demand for labour saving gadgets and for services once performed within the household. However, by the early 1970s, the world economic recession placed a curb on mass production and consumption. Flexible specialization emerged as a viable alternative to the Fordist system of mass production leading to widespread transformations in the world of work and employment. This transformation has far reaching implications for the economic strategies adopted by households and communities.

Of course, even during the post-war boom years of mass production and consumption, household involvement in the formal economy was never total. Fordism was based on the supposed existence of a male-earned family wage that was enough to support a dependent wife and children. Yet as Stanley and Smith (1992) point out, even in Detroit, the presumed bastion of Fordism, the family wage was never a reality for the majority of wage earners. This meant that most households had to implement a complementary mix of formal and informal economic strategies. Stanley and Smith outline the development of household economic strategies in Detroit throughout the 20th century. A brief overview of this account is worth repeating here as it effectively challenges simplistic images of households transforming effortlessly from units of production to units of consumption. If households in Detroit could not rely on the earnings of a single wage earner and therefore had to generate a mixture of strategies to secure economic viability then it is likely that households in other regions less affected by Fordism were likely to implement a complex mix of formal and informal economic activities in order to meet their daily needs.

Stanley and Smith argue that before the second world war, the male wage was supplemented by the wages of children and wives as well as by substantial amounts of subsistence activities. Gardening provided households with a significant portion of their food requirements until after the depression of the 1930s. The keeping of boarders and lodgers also provided households with additional income. The trend towards dependence on male formal employment led to a long-term decline in household size as children moved from being economic assets to becoming economic liabilities. This had a knock-on effect on household subsistence activities as with smaller family sizes, subsistence activities became less economically effective. By the 1950s, households had become increasingly dependent on the wages of a male 'breadwinner' but since the family wage was only a reality for a minority of households, women became increasingly involved in part-time or irregular employment (McGuire and Woodsong, 1992).

The increasing number of women wage earners, particularly married women, enabled households to not only make ends meet but improve their standard of living. In tracing the effects of these changes in New York, Friedman Kasaba (1992) argues that this period was characterized by the increased commodification of household consumption goods. Housework was transformed from the production of domestic goods to the servicing of purchased household commodities. By linking the workings of the household to the revolution in technology, Gershuny (1978) argues that the postwar period has been characterized by the rise of a 'self-service' economy whereby households increasingly substitute internally services once purchased externally in the formal economy. Hence, rather than going to the launderette, individuals buy and use washing machines instead. Of course, the purchase of these appliances led to an increase in the perceived cash needs of the household and this was further enhanced by the ideology of mass consumption nurtured by the Fordist method of production. The ability to purchase these appliances was strongly associated with women's willingness to enter the labour force (Vanek, 1973). Gershuny (1983) went on to elaborate on the importance of this new kind of self-provisioning within the household and this theme was taken up by a number of other writers on the household economy (Burns, 1977; Pahl, 1984; Ironmonger, 1989).

Within this literature, a distinction is made between self-provisioning and conventional housework. The latter term is generally reserved for a limited range of productive work carried out mainly by women within households. These include cooking, cleaning and looking after children and weaker household members. A number of studies have documented how wider structural changes in employment have impacted upon the domestic division of labour within the household. Hudson (1986) for example points out that one of the main responses to the problems inherent in the Fordist method of accumulation was the decentralization of manufacturing production. This resulted in the transfer from skilled or heavy manual work done by men on shifts to semi or unskilled routine assembly work largely undertaken by married women. This rise in formal labour market participation by women was accompanied by a growth in the service sector which created an additional number of gender specific low-grade jobs. Hence the quality of formally available jobs fundamentally changed from traditional, skilled, unionized male manual employment to unskilled, poorly unionized and largely part-time female employment.

These structural changes in the nature of formal employment sparked off a spate of research into the effects of these changes on the domestic division of labour within the household. Unemployed men should have more time on their hands to engage in domestic duties while formally employed wives should have less time. Hence the restructuring of formal employment was considered to pave the way for a renegotiation of domestic roles within the household. However, much of the subsequent research on the domestic division of labour within the household failed to back up this logic. The traditional gendered domestic division of labour survived by and large intact. Husbands helped more in the household, but women continued to undertake a disproportionate share of conventional housework even when they were formally employed in the labour market. Moreover, unemployed males were the group least likely to participate fairly in the domestic division of household tasks.

As far as the economic value of conventional housework is concerned and whether such activities should be considered as part of the formal or informal economy, the discussion centres on the dual role of the household in the realm of production and reproduction. Marxist feminists outline the crucially important role of unwaged labour in the maintenance and reproduction of the workforce. Women in particular play a primary role in the reproduction of labour power through the domestic care of children and adult household members. Apart from reproduction, the household plays an enormous though often invisible economic role in that all of the services performed 'free of charge' within the household have a potential market value. Some economic analyses of traditional housework have attempted to quantify the value of housework by estimating the comparable costs of cooking and cleaning if undertaken through the formal labour market. However, such an approach is fraught with difficulties, not least because of the depressed market value of such formally available services given that they are performed 'free of charge' mainly by women within the household. Nonetheless, some economists argue that if conventional housework was included in national statistics it would fundamentally affect the size of GDP (see Thomas, 1992 for a overview of these statistics).

Most authors have, however, tended to exclude conventional housework from analyses of the informal economy (Warde, 1990) other than focusing on changes in the level of self-provisioning within households. The term self-provisioning is generally utilized to refer to the production of specific goods and services from within the household for consumption by household members. Rather than include all possible forms of housework within this definition, particular goods and services are considered as useful indicators of the extent to which households are substituting for formally produced goods and services. The activities commonly included within this perspective include home baking, home brewing, knitting and dressmaking, hairdressing, general DIY and household maintenance and car repairs. Increases in the provision of such goods and services from within households is regarded as denoting the continuing importance of informal work for the overall economy.

Wheelock (1990) sees changes in the level of self-provisioning within households as one of four possible household adaptations to structural changes in the world of formal employment. Firstly, as the nature of work changes leading to more sporadic, non-standard types of formal employment and widespread unemployment, many households experience a drop in real income and an increase in available time and this encourages participation in informal work and employment practices. In this instance, households may engage in more self-provisioning to replace formally purchased goods and services which become too expensive to obtain. Secondly, households may additionally make use of reciprocal networks to enable them to gain access to scarce goods and resources. Thirdly, unemployed individuals may replace employment in the formal economy with employment in the informal sector of the economy. Finally, poorer households may become purchasers of cheaper informally produced goods and services.

The first two responses lead to opportunities for informal work while the second two lead to opportunities for informal employment. To some extent these two latter responses have been covered indirectly in the previous chapter. The section on the involvement of the unemployed in the informal economy indicated that while some informal employment opportunities do become available, nonetheless the penalties for involvement in countries with highly developed welfare systems may be too severe for the unemployed to implement this option. Moreover, the jobs obtainable tend to be highly exploitative, carried out for extremely low rates of pay and on a very casual basis. Hence from the available evidence, it seems unlikely that informal employment provides any more than a coping strategy for the unemployed rather than a viable alternative to more structured formal employment.

The availability of informal wage labourers operating in the absence of formally binding state legislation and tax laws may indeed be able to supply low income households with cheaper goods and services and hence enable them to gain access to products they otherwise could not afford. Sassen's (1991, 1996) work on the informal economy in the US indicates this trend although her research also shows that more affluent households also make use of the availability of this cheap labour. The section on moonlighting and multiple job holding in the previous chapter outlines some of the groups likely to participate in this practice.

The remainder of this chapter focuses on the first two responses of households to structural economic change outlined by Wheelock. These practices exemplify the resilience of informal unpaid work in an era dominated by wage labour. Self-provisioning within households and reciprocal transactions between households have only recently been included in sociological texts on work although such activities pre-date wage labour and have always co-existed with wage labour. Before turning to an examination of these informal work practices, it is necessary to critically examine the use of the term 'strategy' to explain self-provisioning and the use of the word 'household' to refer to a collection of individuals sharing an occupational residence.

96

Invisible Work, Invisible Workers

HOUSEHOLDS AND STRATEGIES

While the notion that households devise strategies has long occupied the attention of sociologists and economists, it has been suggested that the concept is inappropriate for explaining decision
making within households. Crow (1989) suggests that the concept
is hopelessly imprecise while Edwards and Ribbens (1991) suggest
abandoning the term altogether. The term implies that people within
households get together and rationally calculate the optimum way
in which to deploy the labour of household members. This approach
tends to over emphasize the consensual nature of households and
under emphasize the extent to which households may be sites of
intense conflict and inequality. Hence, by regarding the household
as a single unit, the power imbalances between household members is often obscured. Moreover, there may be significant differences between intended strategies and structural constraints. In other
words, households are often not in a position to freely follow rational intentions. The economic choices that households make may
be prompted through lack of choice rather than the outcome of
decisions between competing choices. While these issues are undoubtedly important, they do not necessarily render defunct approaches which attempt to critically evaluate the diversity of the
nature of work and its link with the formal and informal economy
through the economic strategies of household members.

The review of the literature that follows, on the extent of self-
provisioning strategies within households in an era dominated by
sweeping changes in the world of work and employment, by and
large concentrates on the ways in which households collectively
organize their economic activities through involvement in informal
work strategies. Such approaches recognise the existence of a sexual
division of labour in production within the household in that men
are primarily involved in DIY and general household improvements
while women are involved in knitting, dress-making and other more
domesticated forms of self-provisioning. However, often the existence of this sexual division of labour is not integrated into the
analysis of the mode of production as a whole but merely described
in general terms. Nonetheless, while bearing in mind these criti-
cisms, such an approach enables us to critically evaluate the significance of informal work in the lives of household members.

SELF-PROVISIONING WITHIN HOUSEHOLDS

Self-provisioning refers to the production of goods and services within the household for self-consumption. Hence the products of self-provisioning do not pass through the market. The goods and services produced by self-provisioning are not produced for exchange but rather are concerned with use values. The labour expended is private labour not socialized labour. This is because such labour is not concerned with the buying and selling of commodities through the formal labour market. The structural changes in employment which have characterized advanced industrial capitalism have lead to a reduction in formal employment and an increase in the importance of forms of work based on activities which are often considered non-economic.

Self-provisioning illustrates some of the difficulties involved in identifying just what constitutes work. One approach is to define work by its outcome. Self-provisioning within the household generates a good or service which would otherwise have to be formally purchased. However, Harding and Jenkins (1989) argue that the subjective view of the participant is crucial in defining what is work and what is not. There are conceivably many instances in which these two approaches would not coincide. Take for example, someone who grows enough vegetables to fulfil the household's internal consumption needs but who defines this activity as a pleasurable pastime. Following the first approach, the practice involves a clear substitution for something which would otherwise have to be obtained through the formal market economy and paid for in monetary terms. However, following the second approach, the actor clearly does not define this activity as work. This contradiction illustrates the blurred distinctions which often exist between work and leisure. Ronco and Peattie (1988) suggest that whether an activity is defined as 'work' or as a 'hobby' depends on the social context in which the activity is carried out rather than inherent in the activity itself. However, their own analysis to demonstrate this throws up all sorts of added contradictions. There is no single set of social relations in which work is embedded. Rather there are continually shifting, complex and paradoxical social and economic relationships between people which are in turn shaped and influenced by wider structural forces such as the capitalist economic system and formal labour market and by social hierarchies of age, gender and ethnicity. However, what is clear is that an analysis of economic activity which ignores use value production is inadequate and leads to distortions in the measurement of active labour. Economic activity should be defined in relation to its contribution to the production of goods and services for the satisfaction of human needs regardless of whether this production is channelled through the market or through the household. By treating household work and wage labour as separate issues, the full range of household economic strategies has been blurred and the continued importance of work which takes place outside formal employment has been undermined.

While the internal decision-making processes through which individual household members reach decisions concerning involvement in different work and employment practices have been largely underplayed by researchers into the informal economic aspects of household work strategies, nonetheless there has been some attempt to recognise that households are likely to be very diverse in nature and this undoubtedly would impact on the formal and informal practices implemented. The size, composition and economic status of the household is likely to influence participation in unwaged work. Moreover, households are never fixed but constantly changing entities. Indeed the average person is likely to belong to several different household types in the course of a lifetime. Most of us start out as dependent children within households containing at least one adult. As we reach maturity, we may leave our initial household and join other households or form our own households. The older we become the more likely our households will decrease in size. At each of these various stages of the lifecycle, our involvement in unwaged work within the household is likely to change. From his research into the informal work strategies of households in Italy, Vinay (1985) suggests that a life cycle approach is crucial to examining changes in rates of participation in unwaged household work over time.

Married couples with young dependent children are deemed the most likely to engage in self-provisioning within the household. This is because their needs are likely to be greater and they are also likely to have greater variation in the resources at their disposal. Research by Glatzer and Berger (1988) into levels of self-provisioning in West Germany found that household composition was the most significant factor in accounting for variations in self-provisioning among households and this remained the case when other variables such as income and class were taken into account. The lowest degree of self-support was found in one person households. While often these households lacked sufficient resources to purchase goods and services from the formal market, nonetheless they did not possess sufficient labour power to rely on self-production.

The allocation of time is another crucial factor likely to influence participation in self-provisioning within the household. The time that an individual spends on household production is time that could alternatively been spent on leisure or on employment in the formal economy (Smith, 1986). Since time is a scarcer resource for some individuals compared to others then it seems logical to assume that those with the most time on their hands would be prone to undertaking the most self-provisioning work. Hence, the unemployed should have higher rates of participation compared to the formally employed. However, much of the research does not bear out this conclusion. Pahl (1984) for example, from his research in the UK, differentiated between work-rich and work-poor households. Those with the greatest access to formal employment were likely to engage extensively in self-provisioning within the household as well. This observation has been supported by a number of other studies in other countries (see for example Offe and Heinz, 1992 – West Germany; Sassen, 1996 – US; Mingione, 1988 – Italy).

These studies indicated that informal work within the household needs more than time. It demands skills and money to buy the articles necessary to convert materials into final products. Household income obviously influences the ability of households to purchase formal goods and services. If households can easily afford the formal purchase of goods and services then it seems reasonable that they will have little incentive to engage in self-provisioning. Yet, the studies outlined above indicate that high income households are those most likely to engage in self-provisioning. To some extent this is tied up with home ownership. High income householders tend to own their own homes and thus engage in a wide range of DIY house maintenance and improvement measures.

In attempting to measure the size of the informal economy in Britain, Smith (1986) argues that the key issue in relation to the size of any aspect of the informal sector is the extent of substitution between the formal and informal provision of goods and services. This involves considering on what basis households choose to do something for themselves and to have others done through the formal economy. We have already considered how stages in life-cycle, household composition, income and time impinge on these decisions. Smith (1986:165) suggests that the choice between household and formal economy provision depends on a comparison between the wages that could be earned from formal employment, the 'opportunity cost' of labour time in the household economy and the market price of the service if purchased from the formal economy. However, such an analysis over-emphasizes the extent to which households have choices over these factors. Some groups may be excluded from earning wages in the formal sector and their non-economic status may be enhanced by their inability to afford the resources necessary to engage in home production.

Moreover, Gershuny (1988) reminds us that self-provisioning does not involve total substitution for the formal production of goods and services. Rather unpaid household labour is combined with the formal purchase of materials and equipment necessary for the provision and consumption of final goods and services within the household. Hence, the growth of self-provisioning within the household was accompanied by a boom in the formal DIY industry. For Gershuny (1988), growth in the household economy is encouraged by the rising cost of purchased services relative to the declining costs of domestic capital goods. Employment protection legislation, employers' social security contributions and trade union policies make the supply of formal labour increasingly expensive. It thus becomes economically rational for households to engage in self-provisioning and they are assisted by a wide range of DIY books and equipment which 'de-skill' the tasks involved. This leads to a shift in the production of goods and services from the formal economy to the household economy.

However, it is clear from the above discussion that the ability of households to engage in self-provisioning is not uniform. Self-provisioning costs money and seems to be a strategy implemented by relatively well-off households rather than poorer households. Indeed, Pahl (1984) differentiates between multiple-earner households who engage in a whole host of self-provisioning activities and no-earner households with lots of time on their hands but without the necessary resources to engage in self-provisioning. Smith and Wallerstein (1992:261) regard the first group as the beneficiaries of Fordism. Their combined wages enable them to purchase the mass consumption items whose sale forms a key element of contemporary global profit. But here lies the paradox. The new mass consumption items are sold incomplete and require self-provisioning labour to produce the final item. This means that productive workers not only contribute surplus value once as waged workers but they additionally contribute surplus value as self-provisioning consumers. Moreover, often these self-provisioning activities are redefined as leisure activities thus again indicating the fluid boundaries between work and leisure. To Smith and Wallerstein, much of modern leisure pursuits are in reality self-provisioning labour.

But what about poorer households? Such households often have insufficient access to the resources necessary to adapt unfinished goods through the use of self-provisioning into goods for final consumption. As these households experience a decline in income through less standard forms of employment or through unemployment, they also have to turn to subsistence activities to enable them to maintain an adequate standard of living. However, as these activities have declined in importance due to the previous incorporation of such households into wage labour, then some households are unable to resurrect such activities. Such households become increasingly dependent on welfare handouts and the state to some extent takes over responsibilities once performed by the household. Of course the ability of the state to fulfil the needs of the household by means of its welfare provisions will differ substantially between one country and another. States with generous welfare policies such as France and Germany may enable some households to cope with the insecurity of wage labour opportunities without such households having to implement significant self-provisioning strategies. States with limited welfare policies such as Portugal and Greece may encourage the survival of self-provisioning practices such as subsistence agriculture. Moreover, welfare provision is not fixed but subject to fluctuating political concerns. For example, the new right ideologies which characterized the provision of welfare in the US and the UK in particular over the last decade have involved a dismantling of the welfare state. Households dependent on welfare benefits have increasingly had to resort to a range of informal economic strategies to supplement the growing inadequacy of their welfare benefits entitlements to meet their daily needs.

These households have remained partially self-sufficient by providing food, clothing and shelter for themselves by non-market means. Hence, while the trend towards self-provisioning follows much of what has been outlined in previous paragraphs, a range of locality studies have demonstrated the efforts of poorer households to meet their own needs by relying on the internal resources of the household (see Mingione 1987; McGuire and Woodsong, 1992; Leonard,

1994). These studies indicate that the self-provisioning tasks that were carried out were largely gender-specific. Males were generally involved in minor home improvements and renovations while females generally engaged in knitting and dressmaking. These tasks were not so much related to turning partially completed goods into luxury goods for final consumption by internal family members but with attempting to meet basic needs through self-provisioning. In the absence of the money needed to purchase final goods and services, poorer households relied on the labour of unskilled family members to substitute where possible for the formal purchase of necessary goods and services. However, Offe and Heinze (1996) argue that there are clear limits to the extent of this substitution. Households are generally decreasing in size and this leads to negative economies of scale rendering self-provisioning less and less worthwhile. Hence, poorer households face a constant contradiction between the rationality of increased self-provisioning and a structurally limited capacity to make use of it. Offe and Heinze argue that one solution to these problems is to develop economic links between households. The ability of poorer households to build up economic relationships with other households is the concern of the next section of the chapter.

CROSS-HOUSEHOLD COOPERATION

In an historical account of the family throughout the nineteenth and twentieth centuries, Hareven (1982) outlines the important role that cross-household cooperation played in facilitating the transition to industrial society. The family and larger kinship groups adopted roles as intermediaries between individual members and the factory system in recruiting workers from rural areas, not only during the initial phases of industrialization but throughout the nineteenth and twentieth centuries. Kinship ties and kin assistance was essential to rural labourers' migration to industrial centres and their incorporation into new urban lifestyles. The family and community acted as a buffer zone enabling new recruits to cope with the insecurities of employment and potential threat of unemployment. Kinship and community ties were central in facilitating settlement and adaptation to new employment and living conditions. Living in close proximity to one's kin was a crucial housing strategy as kinship ties could be called upon in times of need. Gradually these bonds of kinship assistance extended throughout the neighbourhood drawing poor people in particular into networks of mutual obligation that enable them to cope with periods of insecurity and need. Hareven (1990) argues that in the absence of social security, these ties represented a crucial source of assistance enabling many households to cope with the insecurities imposed by industrialization. Her research outlines the numerous ways in which households helped other households through loaning money or tools and trading skills, goods and services. Women played a central role in these exchanges particularly in relation to kinship ties where they were the primary 'kin keepers' maintaining ties with kin over the life course (Hareven, 1990:237).

The Fordist system of production did much to undermine the need for households to rely on other households in times of need. As Myles (1990) points out, Fordism was more than simply a production technique. It was constructed around a system of wage stabilization at historically high levels that supposedly eliminated the 'cycle of poverty'. Fordism depended on payments to workers over the life course to enable them to purchase the mass goods produced. This necessitated not just changes in industrial relations practices but also in state policy. Not only was long term employment guaranteed but this was backed by state provision of sickness, unemployment and retirement benefits. These benefits were generally directed at adult males who would have high levels of employment at relatively high wages and would be allowed to retire with a retirement wage. Women and children would be supported through these male wage rates and through the welfare benefits policies to which males were entitled to.

Of course, many individuals remained outside the cushion of the welfare state provisions outlined above. In the United States, for example, only certain workers were able to avail themselves of the Fordist cycle of welfare benefits. Workers in the core mass production industries had access to state social benefits, employer-sponsored, state-subsidized insurance policies and other fringe benefits. Workers not located in core industries received partial, conditional assistance that often failed to cover their everyday needs. In southern European countries such as Greece, where the agricultural sector remained important, the Fordist system of production was the exception rather than the norm and welfare state provisions remained weak and ineffective leaving individuals with little option but to continue to rely on traditional sources of subsistence to meet their household needs.

Moreover, by the 1970s, even countries with universal welfare benefits provisions began a slow process of welfare state erosion (Myles, 1990). Rising unemployment levels in all industrial countries placed unforeseen pressure on the ability of welfare states to meet citizens' needs. Long-term unemployment with the one company was increasingly replaced by sporadic, low-paid forms of employment. Rather than a stop gap measure to cover people's needs during brief periods of employment insecurity, the welfare state emerged as a fundamental component of people's working lives. States coping with prolonged recession, increased competition leading to poorer formal employment opportunities and conditions came to see the welfare state as undermining the incentive to work. As part of a package of restructuring strategies, a number of states including the UK and the USA began a process of dismantling the welfare state.

Local communities often bear the brunt of restructuring (Laws, 1989). The decline in value of wages from formal employment, higher unemployment levels and reductions in welfare state provisions have rekindled interest in the ability of communities to meet shortfalls and absorb potential social problems. While the need to maintain kinship and community ties has considerably lessened particularly among middle class households and while these households are likely to be privatized units of consumption or self-contained, self-provisioning units, nonetheless, among working class and new ethnic households, some of the historical characteristics of exchange networks have persisted although in modified form (Hareven, 1990:241). The persistence and resilience of these community networks have challenged neoclassical economic explanations concerning economic action and led to a resurgence of interest in sociological explanations of economic life.

Portes (1995) argues that traditional economics tends to place little attention on the motives of economic actors to engage in the production of scarce goods and services and the possible social influence of others upon their activities. While economic sociology accepts that actors are rational in terms of pursuing goals through deliberately selected means, nonetheless social relationships permeate every stage of this process. This means that even individuals engaged in the pursuit of selfish ends often have to modify and constrain their pursuits due to their membership in a host of human groups ranging from the household to the community and other associations such as ethnic or religious groupings.

This notion of economic behaviour draws on the concept of embeddedness. This refers to the notion that heterogeneous economic transactions are subject to subtle social structures that often influence their outcomes. The concept originated with the Hungarian anthropologist Karl Polanyi (1957) who suggested that there are three major modes of exchange in human societies; market exchange, redistribution and reciprocity. Market exchange is the subject matter of conventional economics and refers to the exchange of goods and services at prices based on supply and demand. Redistribution involves the gathering of economic goods and services to some central place and then their redistribution throughout the populace. The welfare state can be viewed as a formal system of redistribution while the 'free' distribution of second hand goods such as children's clothes among extended family or community members can be seen as an informal method of redistribution. Reciprocity involves exchanges which lie outside the market calculus. The concept refers to the mutual recognition of the obligation to give and receive and draws economic actors into dense webs of expectations which modifies their ability to selfishly pursue their individual economic interests.

This notion of reciprocity has been adopted as a tool for examining the incorporation of individuals into community networks. These networks enable individuals to gain access to scarce goods and resources while setting in motion reciprocal obligations. According to Abrams (Bulmer, 1986:3), reciprocity is likely to flourish in 'relatively isolated, relatively closed and relatively threatened social milieu with highly homogeneous populations where information and trust are high and where resources for satisfying needs in other ways are low'. The ability of these reciprocal networks to provide individuals with informal work opportunities can be illustrated by examining their prevalence in low income urban areas particularly among ethnic minorities.

One of the most influential studies of how social relationships and networks operate to meet economic needs was carried out by Carol Stack (1974). Her research was located in a community experiencing severe economic depression. The economic insecurity experienced by residents was lessened through their extensive kinship and friendship networks which lessened their dependence on formal sources to meet their daily needs. The most widely practised strategies involved swapping, trading and borrowing from one household to another. In this way, the scarce range of goods available in the community could be redistributed throughout a number of households. Services were also 'swapped'. Hence residents could trade their limited skills with the limited skills of other community members and in the process gain access to a wider range of services than their internal resources could cover. Lowenthal (1981) found a similar range of practices in Boston. Here households engaged in a range of economic transactions that were embedded in networks of social relationships. Households exchanged services such as carpentry, housepainting and help with moving house. Involvement in these exchanges were gender specific with males engaging in visible services such as home improvements and maintenance while females engaged in more intangible exchanges such as caring for the sick, the elderly and children.

A number of more recent studies have backed up these observations (see Leonard, 1992; Morris, 1994; Mingione, 1994b). Sassen (1996) suggests that low income populations need cheap, locally produced goods and services to meet their everyday material needs. While prices may be charged for the provision of such goods and services, prior relationships often influence the pricing mechanism utilized. Moreover, often services and goods are exchanged in kind. This enables those with insufficient monetary resources to participate in the reciprocal exchange of goods and services and hence gain access to a wider range of supplies than their income would allow.

Morris and Irwin (1992) focused on the levels of support among four types of households: couples in which the man was long-term unemployed, couples in which the man was securely employed, couples in which the man was recently recruited to employment and couples in which the man was out of the labour force. Their research concentrated on a number of exchanges including the provision of services such as gardening, home maintenance/repairs, car maintenance/repairs, clothing and financial help relating to loans to get households through to the end of the week, pay bills or buy things for the house or for children. They found that the density of informal support was highest among the long-term unemployed. Much of the support available however depended on kinship rather than friendship ties, although they also found that friendship ties had the potential to develop among long-term unemployed households.

The networks discussed thus far are mainly generated by kinship and community relationships, however, ethnic relationships are also an important consideration. Decisions to migrate are usually made within a collective context that includes the family and local community. As Tilly (1990:84) puts it 'individuals do not migrate, networks do'. Cummings (1980) outlines the ways in which immigrant groups respond collectively to the conditions posed by urban, industrial life. He suggests that ethnic minority groups pursue collective rather than individual modes of economic action. These groups often rely on reciprocal networks in the absence of social services, welfare benefits and access to capital. Often self-help organizations were created to assist newly arrived immigrants with finding employment and housing. This often led to the concentration of ethnic groups within specific occupational sectors. Hence, Italians and Jews became heavily involved in the garment and construction industries while eastern European immigrants became involved in extraction, mining and steel industries (Cummings, 1980:10). Similarly, Bailey and Waldinger (1991) outline how certain ethnic groups became involved in particular industries creating occupational niches for subsequent migrants. While these strategies were aimed at helping subsequent migrants gain formal and informal employment positions, they also set in motion reciprocal work practices aimed at supplementing these other tactics.

Cummings (1980) argues that it is important to not just concentrate on the formal and informal ethnic employment strategies of migrant groups but to examine the totality of their responses to economic uncertainties. Such groups were often able to establish cohesive neighbourhoods and deliver social services to community members. While not every immigrant group organized their economic activities in the same fashion, despite similar historical and cultural experiences, nonetheless, his focus on 13 different immigrant groups to the United States revealed some common themes. Chinese, Greek, Italian, Irish and Jewish immigrants in particular incorporated a whole range of informal work strategies into their economic behaviour. These included the interchange of skills among households in order to enhance access to scarce goods and services. Hence, households performed favours for other households on the understanding that such favours would be reciprocated at some later date. The equivalency of the return was left unspecified locking households into long-term relationships with other households.

Of course, not all low-income communities will have access to informal work opportunities or mutual aid networks. Roberts (1994) for example, suggests that cohesive community based strategies are largely absent in Afro-American ghettoes. Here responses to economic insecurity are individual rather than collective and individuals pursue strategies aimed at maximizing income rather than enhancing community relationships. Wilson's (1993) research in a low income, inner city Indianapolis neighbourhood produced similar negative findings. The everyday reality of sub-standard wages, crumbling housing and poor municipal services produced feelings of powerless and fatalism in residents. These feelings discouraged residents from becoming actively involved in community networks. Most residents held very negative attitudes to their community and their daily lives were conditioned by bleak acceptance of the surrounding deprivation rather than by any attempt to diluted the negative features of their environment. Neef (1992) in an overview of research into community networks in a number of locations in West Germany found similar levels of detachment. Marginalized groups did not openly manifest their poverty but were often ashamed of it and tended to retreat to the privacy of their households rather than engage in any community exchanges with households in similar predicaments. This draws attention to the different manifestations of restructuring both within and between countries.

In a follow-up report to the European Commission's Employment Task Force on the informal economy, Mingione (1994a) focuses on the continued importance of community exchanges and networks in Germany after unification. Quoting from a study carried out by Seifert, Rose and Zapf in 1993, Mingione suggests that exchanges of help among relatives and friends is of greater importance in East than West Germany. Households in rural areas in particular engaged in a wide range of exchange networks. Almost everyone grew vegetables and used their skills to carry out repairs for other households and offered a range of reciprocal services to other households. In a similar vein, Mingione's (1994b) research in Italy demonstrates the different family and community strategies adopted by households in the North of Italy compared to the South. In the North, household and community strategies promote incorporation into both formal and informal employment networks while in the South, these strategies represent little more than subsistence strategies aimed at diluting (often unsuccessfully) the deficiencies of the formal system. These regional variations emphasize the importance of locality in facilitating or hindering the growth of community networks.

The research reviewed here suggests that cultural isolation, long-term stability of residence, social homogeneity, extensive kinship, friendship and ethnic networks and low levels of access to external resources are all conducive to the development of informal work practices (Leonard, 1994). Moreover, self-interest was by no means absent from the exchanges instigated. Most were conditioned by the principle of reciprocity which implied that some sort of return was expected from those for whom favours were performed. Menjivar's (1997) ethnographic fieldwork among Salvadorans in San Francisco indicated that the scarcity of resources and intrinsic economic uncertainty which characterized their daily lives undermined the potential of reciprocal networks developing. The inability of some individuals to reciprocate and hence be left outside these networks indicates the limits of these networks to fully compensate for the failings of the formal economy. This issue is examined in the next section.

CARING COMMUNITIES: FACT OR FANTASY

The increasing pressure on the poor to supplement inadequate welfare entitlements or to generate income in the absence of welfare has led to a renewed interest in family and community strategies as a means of coping with economic uncertainty. Wolch (1989) argues that states throughout the world have a fiscal interest in the caring capacity of communities as a supplement to, or replacement of, state-provided welfare. The restructuring of the welfare state has led to a revival of community strategies aimed at providing substitutions for inadequate or non-existent state care. This retreat of the state through programmes of privatization and cutbacks in welfare expenditure has enhanced the development of 'fragmented societies' (Mingione, 1991) and encouraged the return of forms of work not conventionally considered in texts on the sociology of work (Pahl, 1988). However, it is important not to over-emphasize the importance of these networks for enabling households to cope with the shortfalls in the formal provision of goods and services. While a number of locality studies present accounts of the myriad of often ingenious strategies of households and communities to gain access to scarce goods and resources, the overwhelming conclusion of these studies is that they represent a minor aspect of the economic strategies of individuals, households and communities to meet their daily needs.

Roberts (1991) suggests that there is little evidence to indicate that households and communities can solve their problems through a more skilful management of their own resources. Some aspects of the current restructuring of urban space hinder the creation of the kinds of neighbourhood communities necessary to facilitate communal transfers of resources. For example, redevelopment often destroys stable, working class communities. The relocation of manufacturing industries often leads to urban decay and the 'ghettoization' of the central city. These areas tend to be characterized by isolation and desperation and households turn to crime rather than collective, coping strategies. There are other demographic changes in the composition of households which call into question the capacity of households to enter into reciprocal exchanges with other households.

The literature on the exchanges of goods and services between households highlights reciprocity as the linch pin connecting these transactions. However, reciprocity is often tinged with self-interest and this factor is often ignored in the literature on this area. Reciprocity locks individuals into long standing relationships with other individuals on the principle that 'one good turn deserves another'. Often exchanges are subtle and concerned with different types of goods and services, hence participants are never certain whether or not the favour has been fully repaid. Gouldner (1960) suggests, for example, that once a stable pattern of mutual gratification has been established the system becomes self-perpetuating. Reciprocity induces a certain amount of ambiguity as to whether the favour has been repaid and over time generates uncertainty about who is in whose debt. While exchanges may be unequal at any particular point in time, there is a general recognition that eventually 'balanced' reciprocity will be achieved. This means that individuals are likely to engage in reciprocal arrangements with those they assume will be able to reciprocate at some time in the future. This begs the question – what happens to those unable to reciprocate? There is some evidence to indicate that such individuals are likely to be left outside of these reciprocal networks (Finch, 1993; Leonard 1997). Hence, while reciprocity may well operate as a safety valve in certain circumstances, and enable some households to gain access to goods and services otherwise unavailable, it may well induce the neglect of those unable to maintain reciprocal relationships. Since recent demographic trends indicate an aging population and a rise in the number of single parent/person households in most cities of the developed world, then the ability of reciprocal community networks to cover the shortfall engendered by restructuring seems severely limited.

NETWORKS: WORK AND EMPLOYMENT

Some of the activities outlined by the research into the exchange of goods and services in low income communities vary little from the informal employment activities discussed in the previous chapter. Moonlighters may provide services on an informal basis to a wide variety of individuals outside their kinship and community networks. Sassen (1996) for example suggests that high income gentrification creates a demand for goods and services that are not mass produced or sold through mass outlets. Such speciality items and services may be provided at a lower price by the informal labour power of off-the-books workers. Moonlighters may charge lower prices for the goods and services which they supply through labour additional to their primary occupation. Similarly, the unemployed may engage in such activities and conceal the income earned from the relevant authorities. These individuals may also supply their own networks with goods and services and may place a monetary value on their work effort. However, as the previous discussion indicated, this value is unlikely to be fixed but to fluctuate because of the influence of social relationships on these exchanges.

The importance of social factors and relations on individuals' economic behaviour has been traditionally ignored in conventional economics. The relationships between community members engaged in these exchanges are qualitatively different from the relationships between labourers and employers/customers outlined in the previous chapter. This applies even when money forms the basis of the exchange. Consumer demand depends on the wants and needs of the community and hence to a certain extent constitutes a protected market. Production and exchange is locally based and dependent on kinship and community ties. These ties profoundly influence the economic behaviour of participants. Goods and services are not always sold at their potential price; instead pricing is influenced by the relationship between trading partners. Hence the pursuit of material gain interacts with community relationships and impedes the ability of individuals to maximize their economic gain. This makes it difficult to estimate the economic value of such exchanges. Arriving at calculations based on the comparable value of the labour involved if such goods and services were formally purchased ignores the extent to which individuals' economic behaviour is influenced by social concerns.

Where money does not change hands, the economic value of exchange is even more difficult to establish. Often conventional economics excludes unpaid activities from their remit by assuming that such activities are non-economic and do not constitute proper work. This undermines the labour effort that often accompanies such exchanges. While economists may find it relatively easy to estimate the economic value of informal labour involved in the production of goods or tangible services, it is more difficult to place an economic estimate on the revival of caring communities. Often caring for others involves intangible activities and invokes a concept of 'love labour' which generally lies outside the estimates of the value of work and employment undertaken by conventional economics.

Wolch (1989) argues that the restructuring of capitalist states has resulted in massive transformations in states' responsibilities for population welfare. She documents the rise of a 'shadow' welfare state based on transferring responsibilities for citizens on to the voluntary sector. While this strategy has created formal job opportunities for individuals in the voluntary sector on a paid or unpaid basis, it also depends to a substantial extent, on the invisible work efforts of individuals within households and communities. Conventional economics is still a long way from fully recognizing the extent of this labour let alone developing the economic indicators appropriate for evaluating the economic significance of such work.

6 Women and the Informal Economy

The informal economy is a gender neutral term which covers the work of both sexes but often conceals an internal sexual division of labour. From a review of studies into participants in the informal economy, Hoyman (1987) suggests that women's involvement is likely to exceed that of men. She argues that barriers to women's participation in the formal economy are likely to push women towards the informal economy. This means that many women end up in the informal economy out of necessity rather than choice. The occupations that women fill in the informal economy are likely to mirror those of the formal economy thus the informal economy often reinforces the inferior status of women.

The historical separation of work from employment, outlined in Chapter 3, had a fundamental impact on women's economic lives both within and outside the household. The rise of industrial capitalism separated the 'female' household from the 'male' economy. Women's subsequent disproportionate responsibility for unpaid housework and childcare had a fundamental impact on availability for paid employment outside the household. The paid economic activities of men were elevated at the expense of the unpaid economic activities of women and the conventional economic accounting procedures which emerged devalued the economic contributions of women to the overall economy. Since the post-war period, women are entering the wage labour force in increasing numbers throughout Europe and the US. However, they do so under conditions less favourable than men. They are often paid less for similar tasks or are concentrated in low-paid, gender specific activities. Their ability to earn income is often fragmentary and irregular being closely bound up with their responsibilities within the household. This makes women ideal recruits for the informal employment practices that accompany the trend towards greater flexibility of the labour market. Industrial restructuring, the decentralization of capital and movement towards flexible accumulation do not have impartial effects on the labour market. Rather such processes shape and are shaped by conventional gender stereotypes. This chapter seeks to

113

illustrate this issue by focusing on the gender dimension of informal employment.

It is important to note from the outset that women in Europe and the US do not form a homogeneous group. Class and ethnicity, for example, are likely to have a fundamental impact on women's life chances. However, a number of common patterns and experiences characterize their involvement in informal employment. These include: the neglect of women in conventional economic analyses of active labour; the gender-specific effects of the inter-relationship between the household and the labour market; the survival of patriarchal ideologies which enable males to exploit the labour supply of female family members and the resilience of ideologies which justify the inclusion of women into a restructured labour market through non-standard employment. The chapter is structured around these themes.

WOMEN'S ECONOMIC ROLES WITHIN AND OUTSIDE THE HOUSEHOLD

Before the rise of industrial capitalism, both productive and reproductive labour involved unpaid activities within the household and community. While men and women engaged in different tasks, the economic contributions of both were considered vital to the economic potential of the household. As paid employment increased in importance, unpaid forms of work decreased in value and were considered as marginal to economic life. While many women did play a significant role in wage labour, their primary association with the domestic sphere of reproduction allowed men to gain a dominant position in the formal arena of production (Milkman and Townsley, 1994). Industrial capitalism was accompanied by the cultural construction of an ideology of domesticity whereby housework and childcare came to be regarded as the 'natural' vocation of women. As industrialization progressed, more and more women entered the formal labour market. However, they continued to principally assume responsibility for housework and childcare on an unpaid basis within the household. They also entered the labour market on terms separate from and unequal to that of men being delegated to low-paid jobs in specific occupations that gradually became defined as 'female' work.

Because women continued to perform housework and childcare for 'free' within the household, this depressed the market value of similar activities performed in the formal economy such as cooking, cleaning and childcare. Such jobs became characterized as unskilled, low-paid and overwhelmingly attracted female participants. The rise of the service sector ushered in a host of new occupations that came to be seen as extensions of women's roles within the household and women began to dominate those aspects of the service sector which involved looking after the needs of others. The US Department of Labour (1991) estimates that more than half of all women workers are employed in clerical, sales and service work where pay and status are undervalued and opportunities for advancement are almost non-existent. A report on women and work in Europe (Bulletin, 1994) found that women in the majority of European countries were segregated in low-paid, low-status female dominated occupations. The segregation of the labour market on the basis of gender remains a key obstacle to the achievement of equality in employment opportunities and conditions for men and women in Europe and the US.

While advances in technology removed some of the labour intensive aspects of domestic labour, rising expectations and higher living standards meant that such advances had a minimal impact on the time women continued to spend on household work. Their participation in waged employment outside the household also had little influence on their responsibility for housework. Women in paid employment do spend less time on average on housework compared to full-time housewives, nonetheless their contribution in relation to other family members remains substantial (Hartmann, 1981). A range of studies has indicated that while men may participate more in housework than in the past, particularly if their wives are involved in full-time paid employment outside the household, nonetheless parity remains a long way off (see Pleck, 1995 for a review of this literature). Housework and childcare remain disproportionately female responsibilities and continue to significantly influence the conditions under which women become available for paid employment outside the household (Milkman and Townsley, 1994).

The incorporation of women into the formal wage economy has coincided with an expansion in part-time employment in Europe and the US. Part-time employment is considered as an ideal option for women with family responsibilities as it enables them to merge domestic responsibilities with their desire or need to obtain paid work outside the household. Such jobs are generally inferior to comparable full-time jobs in terms of hourly rates of pay, job security and employment conditions. Fagan and Rubery (1996) found that while part-time work is not necessarily a prior condition for the mobilization of women into the wage economy for European women, nonetheless, women account for a substantial percentage of part-time workers in all EU member states ranging from 65 per cent in Greece to 91 per cent in Germany. In relation to the US, Callaghan and Hartmann (1991) found that 66 per cent of all part-time workers were female. Fagan and Rubery also found that women in part-time work were more likely to be employed in highly feminized occupations compared to full-time workers. While their analysis revealed different levels for different countries, nonetheless, the general trend was for part-timers to be disproportionately present in 'feminized service jobs in all countries' (1996:244). Dex and Walters (1989) from a comparison of women's occupational status in Britain, France and the US found that the creation of part-time female jobs was closely associated with occupational downgrading.

The vulnerable kinds of employment that exist for women in the formal economy make women particularly susceptible recruits for employers seeking to maximize flexibility in an increasingly competitive and volatile marketplace through the creation of informal types of employment. While an overview of all possible forms of informal employment and their gendered nature lies outside the scope of this chapter, a focus on the decentralization of production giving rise to a growth in sweatshops and industrial homeworking succinctly illustrates some of the ways in which women are drawn into informal wage labour doing jobs that enhance traditional assumptions about women and work in modern society. Before turning to specific examples, it is necessary to examine the distorted ways in which women are treated in conventional analyses of women's active labour.

WOMEN'S ACTIVE LABOUR AND CONVENTIONAL ECONOMICS

Since most of women's labour takes place outside the formal market economy, then it is likely that official statistics on active labour will underestimate the economic value of women's contribution to the economy. Women's unpaid domestic labour for example is often excluded from national measures of economic activity such as Gross National Product. Hoyman (1987:72) quotes one study which estimates that if the value of women's work in the household was incorporated into global estimates of GNP, it would raise the value of the world's GNP by as much as one third. Milkman and Townsley (1994) argue that household-based economic production is often neglected in conventional economics as is the possibility that markets, trade-unions, corporations and nation states may operate in a gender-specific manner. They suggest that recognizing the significance of gender does not simply mean including women in standard economic analyses but necessitates revising basic analytical categories such as market, workplace, household and economy.

Beneria (1988) suggests that conventional labour force concepts are concerned with measuring labour participation in commodity production. This single-minded approach ignores the nature and significance of non-commodity production and its role within the economic system. Since women are more likely to engage in non-commodity production compared to men then this leads to a gross undervaluation of women's work and its contribution to the overall economy. Because active labour is defined in terms of the production of exchange values then women's primary involvement in use value production is regarded as marginal or peripheral to the workings of the wider economy. Beneria suggests that active labour should be redefined to include the production of goods and services for the satisfaction of human needs. Such an approach would counteract distortions in the measurement of the labour force which give an incomplete picture of the nature and extent of women's involvement in the economy and would challenge ideological biases relating to the unimportance of women's work emanating from this omission.

'Bringing women in' to economic sociology necessitates rethinking conventional economic categories so that they reflect the economic reality of both men's and women's working lives. This not only involves a re-examination of women's productive role within the household but also their involvement in informal types of paid employment. As Hoyman (1987:82) puts it, 'women's contribution to the informal economy is so dramatic – although invisible – that if ever recorded, it would usher in a new chapter in the book of women in the workforce'. It is to an illustration of some of these informal employment practices that we now turn.

WOMEN AND INFORMAL EMPLOYMENT: FLEXIBLE WORKERS AND FLEXIBLE STRATEGIES

Chapter 3 outlined the decline in the importance of the Fordist mass production methods that characterized the industrial systems of western Europe and the US and how this gave rise to an expansion (or revival) of production activities based on less rigid, more flexible technological and institutional structures (Scott, 1988). This shift has provoked a heated debate concerning the supposed dominance of Fordism during the period 1920–70 and the supposed dominance of flexible specialization since that period (see Nielsen 1991 for an overview of this debate). A number of commentators conclude that while both types of production method are likely to co-exist, the importance of flexible specialization has increased since the 1970s although a complex mix of other production techniques remains important. Often these arguments are presented at a macroeconomic level and the strategies of employers in organizing the production process are given exaggerated coverage at the expense of the effects of their strategies on the workforce. Flexibility in the organization of production creates, sustains and depends on flexibility in labour markets. Moreover, flexible specialization strategies do not have gender-neutral effects on the labour force. The successful implementation of flexible specialization often depends on an ideological construction of women as unpaid wives and homemakers who can be encouraged to engage in income-producing activities that are temporary, part-time, unprotected, non-unionized, and without benefits or state regulation. In other words, flexible specialization often reinforces gender inequalities and this can be illustrated by examining the gendered effects of the growing trend towards subcontracting resulting in an increase in sweatshops and homeworking.

Subcontracting refers to an arrangement whereby an enterprise 'requests another independent enterprise to undertake the production or carry out the processing of a material, component, part or sub-assembly for it according to the specifications or plans provided by the firm offering the subcontract' (Holmes, 1986:84). This strategy particularly appeals to employers with a core of skilled, high-wage workers but who also have a demand for various low-skilled types of work. Unskilled and semi-skilled labour intensive aspects of the production process are farmed out to small-scale workshops who often employ marginal groups of workers such as immigrants and women on a casual, part-time or temporary basis. The subcontracting workshops are not necessarily informal, some may be registered and employ an amalgamation of formal and informal wage labourers. The advantages for the flexible firm are clear. Products with unpredictable demand can be subcontracted thus the number of directly employed workers is cut substantially. Whether or not workers are employed formally or informally is left to the discretion of the subcontractor. Mattera (1985:38) suggests that subcontracting allows larger companies to 'keep their hands clean and let smaller, shady firms do the dirty work of running sweatshops and home work operations'.

Subcontractors predominate in industries which typically employ women such as cleaning, clothing, knitwear, footwear and leather goods. Studies of the gendered nature of the informal economy in the United States often focus specifically on female workers in sweatshops connected to the garment industry (Boris, 1988; Dangler, 1986, Feagin and Smith, 1987). According to Morokvasic (1987) women make up about 80 per cent of the labour force in the garment sector in most industrialized countries and the industry is characterized by the unpredictability and versatility of its market products, small-scale production units and an intricate system of subcontracting. Portes and Sassen-Koob (1987) cite a number of factors responsible for the growth in sweatshops including the pressure international competition puts on reducing indigenous wage levels giving increased opportunities to small-scale employers who are often able to achieve lower wage costs through the creation of informal employment. Sassen-Koob (1984) views sweatshop workers as a particularly effective example of what she terms 'downgraded labour'. Such work is characterized by exploitation, vulnerability, declining relative wages and poorer working conditions. Other studies from southern European countries back up these observations. Hadjimichalis and Vaiou (1990) argue that women's employment in the clothing sector in Greece takes place largely in small-scale, usually unregistered workshops. While Meulders and Plasman (1989) found that throughout southern Europe, the employment of women in sweatshops and other types of feminized atypical employment was the norm.

Benton (1990) traces the extensive shift of certain industries in Spain to the underground economy in order to counteract the shift of production to developing countries. In order to remain competitive in the wake of the growing use of cheap 'third world' labour, many Spanish industries decentralized production. Women were recruited into these smaller informal enterprises because they presented employers with a cheap source of labour and were less likely to engage in collective organization compared to male workers. Lobo (1990a) argues that decentralization and subcontracting from large to small firms have considerably accelerated the segmentation of the labour market. In the toymaking and footwear industries of Valencia, more than 90 per cent of firms use the informal labour of women. Lobo suggests that the irregular work of women in some industries exceeds that of women's legal work. Small scale workshops and sweatshops absorb low-paid female labour and avoid the ever-reaching arm of the state by operating informally and hence avoiding taxation, the enforcement of safety and insurance legislation and collective bargaining agreements.

In relation to West Germany, Frobel, Heinrichs and Kreye (1980) argue that by the 1970s many clothing firms had seized upon the possibility of reducing labour costs by shifting the most labour intensive stages of production to low-wage developing countries. By 1975, this strategy had been adopted by the majority of West German clothing firms. This was mainly due to the high cost of indigenous labour and to the fact that the constantly changing product made further mechanization of production too risky. Hence, savings could only be achieved by using cheap foreign labour rather than through further mechanization. However the need for the clothing industry to locate close to increasingly fashion conscious western markets has reversed this trend and more and more West German clothing firms are turning to the availability of cheap domestic labour. As in the cases outlined above, this labour tends to be predominately female labour particularly from minority groups. Mitter (1986) outlines a similar trend in the UK clothing industry where subcontractors enable retailers to gain access to suppliers who can modify orders on demand. She states (1986:46) 'Flexibility of supply – the capacity to fulfil orders at short notice and the capacity to change an order with a minimum time-lag – gives the domestic suppliers a competitive edge over their overseas counterparts'. Hence, the availability of women willing to work for low wages provides employers with opportunities to bring labour intensive production 'home' to the developed world.

GENDER AND ETHNICITY

A number of studies into the relocation of labour intensive work through subcontracting have made a link between gender and ethnicity to explain the availability of a cheap, docile, domestic labour force. Women from minority backgrounds are doubly disadvantaged in the formal labour market and often become willing recruits for the informal employment practices that often accompany subcontracting. Phizachlea (1987) compares the restructuring of the British and West German clothing industry and the differing impact restructuring had on the employment of minority women workers. She points out that the clothing industry in both countries traditionally relied on immigrant female labour. However, both industries responded differently to the problems of international competitiveness that they each confronted by the late 1960s. West German manufacturers began to exploit the labour cost advantages of the new international division of labour by subcontracting work *externally* to low-wage countries whereas British manufacturers maintained flexibility by subcontracting *internally* to small-scale, inner city firms dominated by ethnic entrepreneurs and labour.

Among the factors Phizacklea cites to explain these separate tactics were the different immigration policies in both countries whereby immigrant entrepreneurs in Britain were able to rely on the labour power of women family members whereas in West Germany, since family reunion was positively discouraged by state legislation, opportunities for immigrant males to rely on their wives' labour power were much more limited. In West Germany, minority women have borne the brunt of job losses due to the relocation of the clothing industry and as a result were pushed to the margins of labour intensive service work, often in the informal sector. By contrast, minority women in the UK found themselves absorbed into the subcontracted sector of clothing production and played a key role in the restructuring of the UK clothing industry.

It is clear from Phizacklea's comparison of the UK and West Germany that men play a fundamental role in facilitating the use of women's labour power. As Phizacklea's research indicates, ethnic business is predominately male business where men are the entrepreneurs and women are the workers. This link is further emphasized by Hoel (1982) who points out that the most successful ethnic groups are characterized by patriarchal social structures which give access to female labour subordinated to patriarchal control mechanisms.

122   *Invisible Work, Invisible Workers*

FLEXIBILITY AND PATRIARCHY

The control of women's labour power by men as well as by capitalists dominates the literature on homeworking among minority women.
Mitter (1986) and Phizacklea (1990) have demonstrated how recession, redundancy and racial discrimination in employment have
coerced a substantial number of ethnic minority men into entrepreneurship in the clothing industry. These ethnic businesses are
able to gain a competitive edge over their rivals because of their
ability to draw on the very cheap labour of female family members.

The extent of men's control over women's labour has also been
applied to the experiences of indigenous women workers in a number of European countries. Lever (1988) outlines the development
of the embroidery industry in Spain whereby large retail companies
subcontract to small local firms which in turn put work out to homeworkers. These homeworkers are mainly women living in rural areas
where opportunities for alternative paid employment are low. Her
account indicates that in its initial stages, the embroidery industry
was dominated by women entrepreneurs. However, control of the
industry gradually passed to men. Among the reasons Lever cites for
this transfer of control were Franco-regime policies designed to keep
Spanish women at home coupled with the reluctance of men to take
on responsibility for domestic work and childcare. Hence, the interests
of the state and men coincided to keep women within the home.

Lever outlines how Spanish men had traditionally found employment in agriculture. However, as opportunities to make a living
from agriculture declined and real wages fell and unemployment
grew, men turned to helping their wives by cutting the cloth, giving out and collecting work and ironing the finished product (which
ironically came to be regarded as a skilled task). The movement
from farming to embroidery initially affected only landless labourers
who were most affected by the recession in agriculture. However
as the crisis in farming intensified, more well-off male farmers began
to transfer their resources into the embroidery industry assisted in
the process by the unpaid labour of their wives and daughters.
Eventually men came to dominate entrepreneurial positions.

While Lever points out that embroidery is obviously skilled work,
male employers and husbands often do not recognize the skills
involved because they rarely have to provide any training. Rather
skills are passed from mothers to daughters and then appropriated
by male entrepreneurs. Lever (1988:18) quotes one entrepreneur

as saying 'embroidery is not proper work because it is done in a woman's free time, between tending to the children'. Yet this non-work of women has enabled many men to benefit substantially from their wives employment in the home and in some cases enabled them to improve their class position.

From her research into immigrants in the Parisian garment industry, Morokvasic (1987) found that men were more likely to have access to entrepreneurship precisely when they did not have any skills in sewing. While Morokvasic's study included women entrepreneurs, these workers were likely to be very highly skilled compared to male entrepreneurs. However, their ability to become successful entrepreneurs was limited due to two factors. Firstly and most importantly, they were unable to rely on the underpaid labour or emotional and practical support of male family members and secondly they often had to rely on men to negotiate their transactions with male retailers and wholesalers. Men, by contrast, were able to rely on the underpaid or unpaid labour power of female family and community members in order to accumulate capital. Because men were able to rely on the cheap, often highly skilled but undervalued labour of female family members, they were able to maintain a degree of success despite their lack of skills. Their 'natural authority' in the family was transferred to the production unit and although these entrepreneurs through time recruit female workers beyond the family unit, they continue to rely on paternalistic types of relationships within their wider kinship network.

Mitter (1986) found similar patterns in the UK clothing industry while Simmons and Kalantaridis (1995) found that in rural Greece, interactions between owners, family members and wage workers were primarily conditioned by the pervading influence of domestic practices and ideologies. In both these case studies, the success of male entrepreneurs depended on their ability to exploit their wives labour power. Patriarchal control in the workplace was linked to patriarchal control generally and men used their patriarchal authority to structure and control their wives labour output by trapping them in low-paid homework.

WOMEN AND HOMEWORKING

Homework is often seen as the logical extension of sweatshops. However, this approach dilutes the diversity of homeworking

124   *Invisible Work, Invisible Workers*

experiences. Homeworking refers to a very heterogeneous range of working practices and groups of people. Many men are also homeworkers and many white collar occupations have been relocated within the home. Allen and Wolkowitz (1987) stress the importance of differentiating between types of home-based work by emphasizing distinctions in terms of the social relations of employment. Hence in their analysis, they exclude domestic labour, self-provisioning and production for barter. Rather they suggest that homeworking must be examined as 'waged labour incorporated into capitalist relations of production'. However rather than lump all forms of wage labour together, they further differentiate between people in professional, managerial and routine white collar occupations and those employed in low-skilled, manufacturing and service occupations. Allen (1996) points out that these types of home-based employment are different in so many respects that it makes more sense to separate them analytically. Following Allen's distinctions, I would suggest that informal employment practices are more likely to be prevalent among low-skilled manufacturing homework compared to professional, managerial and white collar home-based employment. Silver (1989), from a review of homeworkers in the United States, found that homeworkers were in demand disproportionately by the peripheral sector of the economy. Three out of every four homeworkers worked in the periphery, where greater competition, more labour intensive production and lower wages and benefits were the rule. She suggests that international competition promotes market segmentation and the decentralization of production intensifies the demand for homeworkers by the more insecure firms of the periphery sector. The vast majority of homeworkers in these types of enterprises are women who work at home because of inadequate childcare facilities or the entrenchment of patriarchal attitudes that reinforce their 'natural' roles as mothers and housekeepers.

The appeal of homework is often based on the perception of autonomy for those who choose it. In theory, working at home seems to enable the worker to control her own time, choose her own pace and be free from direct supervision. However, in practice, the reality is very different. In order to achieve a level of occupational security, the homeworker has to constantly accommodate the demands of home-life to the demands of the employer. Costello (1988) found that many women encountered severe difficulties in balancing homework and family demands. While some homeworkers received help from their husbands with children and housework, most homeworkers retained primary responsibility for the household. Housework and childcare tasks were added to homework creating a very lengthy working day. Sometimes homework caused conflict with spouses. Some of the men in Costello's study demanded that the homework be completed before they arrived home for dinner.

While inadequate childcare provisions are often given as a primary reason for women engaging in homework, Christensen (1988) suggests that the issue of elder care is likely to assume major proportions over the next few decades as western economies face ageing populations. Homework may emerge as a likely option for women, not only trying to reconcile the demands of housework and childcare but care for the elderly as well. These competing demands between home-life and homework are particularly stressful for workers who are paid on a piece-rate basis as there is a constant tendency to sacrifice family needs in order to meet orders. Payment is often unpredictable and unreliable. Homeworkers often experience extreme isolation and work in circumstances that flout health and safety laws. Many are employed informally, hence the employer evades the payment of social security and other taxes and as a result many homeworkers are not entitled to any employment benefits such as sick pay, redundancy, and other occupational rights.

Dangler (1994) views homeworking as a structural feature of the modern economy. She argues that homeworking forms an essential element of the complex and varying patterns of industrial restructuring that are central to modern capitalism. Homeworking links women in core, semiperipheral and peripheral countries through a global production system into a specific type of employment practice. Often the employer or subcontractor supplies the raw materials needed in production. The homeworkers have no control over what is produced, what wage rates are, and where and how products are marketed. All these decisions, including marketing and selling the final product, are made by the employer. Converting in-house employment to homework results in a significant reduction of many of the risks and uncertainties employers face. Hiring homeworkers enables employers to respond to fluctuations in the market without leaving invested capital idle. Employers usually only pay for correctly completed products and this reduces their potential losses from wasted materials. The often informal status of many homeworkers also enables employers to escape from the need to comply with labour contracts and this further enhances the flexibility of the workforce.

From a review of studies into homeworking in the United States, Silver (1989) found that many undocumented immigrants end up working at home. For example, thousands of Hispanic and Asian homeworkers were found stuffing circuit boards in Silicon Valley and were paid off-the-books. Subcontractors in San Francisco's Chinatown had set up hundreds of garment sweatshops from which approximately half the employees took work home to evade union rules. The California state labour department investigating violations of its homework laws estimated that there were at least 40 000 illegal homeworkers in Los Angeles alone. Similarly, the New York state labour department found that in 1980 there were approximately 50 000 illegal homeworkers in New York city (Silver, 1989:111). Undocumented immigrants can enhance their invisibility by working from home. However, their illegal position makes them an easily exploitable workforce that can be brought in and laid off to accommodate industries with fluctuating demand. Du Rivage and Jacobs (1989) suggest that homeworking contributes significantly to the growing marginalization of the workforce in the United States. Desperate to improve productivity in a stagnant economy, firms subcontract labour intensive aspects of production out to homeworkers who are predominately female, receive low wages and lack fringe benefits and job security. Their research also found that many homeworkers tend to be employed informally rather than formally.

Fernandes-Kelly and Garcia (1989a) remind us that the meaning of homework is likely to vary with the economic, political and social context of women's lives. Hence this type of informal economic activity is often characterized by a considerable degree of internal variation. To illustrate this point, Fernandes-Kelly and Garcia compare the experiences of Hispanic women homeworkers in Miami and Los Angeles. Both locations contain some of the fastest growing Hispanic populations in the United States and make extensive use of the availability of Hispanic labour. Seventy-five per cent of the workforce of garment manufacturers in Los Angeles are Mexican women while 95 per cent of the workforce of apparel manufacturers in Miami are Cuban women. Both locations are also characterized by the co-existence of large industries and small manufacturing operations that escape government regulation. However, despite these similarities, Hispanic women have been drawn into the labour market as homeworkers in differing ways. In Los Angeles, Mexi-

can women immigrants entered the labour force in a highly atom-
ized manner and were at the mercy of market forces beyond their
control. Their undocumented immigrant status, gender and household constraints accentuated their vulnerability and their experiences of homework were characterized by entrenched exploitation.
In Miami, by contrast, Cuban women formed part of an ethnic enclave
dominated by Cuban entrepreneurs. This enabled women from the
same families and communities to use homework as a strategy for
improving earnings and for reconciling home and work demands.

In both regions, households and families played a fundamental
role in allocating women to different segments of the labour market (Fernandez-Kelly and Garcia, 1989b). Both Mexican and Cuban
women sought to obtain homework as a way of combining the responsibilities of family and domestic care with the need to earn a
wage. However, differences in class background and household
composition led to Mexican and Cuban women having contrasting
experiences of homeworking. The absence of an ethnic enclave in
Los Angeles intensified familial conflict within Mexican households.
While Mexican men prized the notion of family life, based on their
role as main providers with women as principal caretakers of children, their inability to obtain employment resulted in their wives
entering the labour market often as undocumented workers in sweatshops. This scenario often militated against the maintenance of
patriarchal standards within the household and as a result many
Mexican women were deserted by their husbands. As a result of
this desertion, the vulnerability of women's positions in the labour
market intensified and many women had no option but to transfer
their paid employment from outside the household to within the
home. Fernandez-Kelly and Garcia argue that in general, homeworking
for Mexican women is a measure of last resort and represents their
attempts to stay a step above poverty.

Cuban women, by contrast, turned to homeworking in much more
favourable circumstances. They entered an entrenched economic
enclave that operated as a buffer zone shielding members of the
same ethnic group from the market forces at play in the broader
economy. Their ability to find employment in garment factories
subsidized the entrepreneurial plans of their husbands. While Cuban women toiled for long hours in factories, their husbands entered the world of business. Eventually they were able to purchase
homes, put their children through school and achieve relatively
comfortable lifestyles. However, at this point, wives employment

outside the household became a stumbling block to the maintenance of patriarchal values based on women's primary role as carers of other family members and men encouraged wives to give up employment altogether or transfer production to home-based units. The shortage of other skilled garment workers in Miami meant that employers had little option but to accommodate this change and enabled women to use homeworking as a strategy for maintaining or improving earnings.

Hence while Cuban women were able to play a fundamental role in enhancing the economic positions of their households, it is clear from the above analysis that involvement in paid employment outside the household did little to undermine the patriarchal dominance of their male partners. The words of one Cuban woman interviewed by Fernadez-Kelly and Garcia (1989a:177) are worth repeating here:

> For six long years I worked in the factory, but when things got better financially, Manolo (her husband) asked me to quit the job. He felt bad that I couldn't be at home all the time with the children. But it had to be done. There's no reason for women not to earn a living when necessary. But I tell my daughters that the strength of a family rests on the intelligence and work of women. It is foolish to give up your place as a mother and a wife only *to take orders from men who aren't even part of the family*. What's so liberated about that? (my emphasis).

Hence while the favourable employment opportunities for Cuban women paved the way for greater personal autonomy and financial independence, the resilience of patriarchal values and their commitment to such values enhanced women's vulnerability rather than strength in both the home and the labour market.

States through their legislative role in regulating labour can have a substantial impact on the characteristics of the informal economy. For example, I have already suggested that the same activity might be part of the formal economy in one country and part of the informal economy in another. This can be illustrated by looking at homeworking in the UK. Hakim (1989) questions the implicit acceptance of the view that since much of homeworking is invisible, it must be illegal as well. She suggests that due to the relatively unregulated labour market in the UK, there has been a legal expansion of part-time, temporary, casual jobs including homeworking. Drawing on the 1981 National Homeworking Survey, Hakim argues that the majority of homeworkers earn wages below the tax and National Insurance thresholds, hence their status as informal workers is questionable. However, a more recent survey of homeworkers in Britain (Felstead and Jewson, 1996) revealed that nine out of ten homeworkers did not have a written contract of employment outlining their terms and conditions of employment; two thirds did not receive an itemized pay slip; three quarters were paid in cash and one fifth had suffered accidents or injuries at work without receiving any compensation. Moreover, very few homeworkers reported that they were entitled to any fringe benefits. Only 7 per cent were entitled to sick pay, only 6 per cent were entitled to holiday pay, only 1 per cent were entitled to redundancy pay and only 1 per cent had a pension scheme. Hence, while the UK government may have facilitated the legal employment of homeworkers, their working conditions remain highly precarious and unfavourable compared to workers employed outside the household. Allen and Wolkowitz (1987:164) argue that although attempts to deregulate the labour market are seen as progressive and represent 'modernization', ironically they frequently involve a return to 'methods of production previously discussed as archaic'.

In reviewing state regulation in the United States, Dangler (1994) found that support for the deregulation of homework was based on the mistaken assumption that homeworkers were independent self-employed workers who did not require the same legal protections guaranteed to factory or office workers. Supporters of deregulation argue that monitoring and regulating the United States' home workforce curbs personal freedom and entrepreneurship and prevents homeworkers with opportunities to gain lucrative and fulfilling work experiences. This conservative approach found expression in the Regan Administration's successful attempt to repeal six of the Fair Labour Standards Act Prohibitory Orders which had banned homework in specific industries since the 1940s. In 1984, the Regan Administration lifted the ban on industrial homework in the knitted outwear industry. In 1988, the bans on homeworking in gloves and mittens, embroidery, buttons and buckles, handkerchiefs and jewelry were lifted. However, opponents of these policies argue that deregulating homework rather than encouraging entrepreneurship cheapens labour and inhibits unionization. Trade union leaders view homework as essentially exploitative because it leads to the widespread violation of labour laws and is often used to weaken or bust unions. Hence, unions in the United States advocate a complete ban on homework as the only solution to combating the oppressive conditions which often accompany this type of employment.

While the UK is likely to have a smaller informal economy compared to other European countries and this is likely to be the case for some types of precarious workers in the United States because of 'legalized deregulation' (Pahl, 1990), nonetheless, homeworkers in Britain and the United States share many similarities with homeworkers in other European countries. They form a cheap, unprotected and highly disposable workforce. The availability of such a workforce has become a pre-condition for the survival of many small-scale subcontractors who remain able to compete through the usage of the extremely cheap labour of women who find access to the external labour market difficult.

OTHER TYPES OF INFORMAL EMPLOYMENT

There are a number of other ways in which women are drawn into the informal economy. Tuominen (1994) estimates that as much as 75 per cent of childcare in the US occurs in the informal sector. Indeed Nelson (1988) suggests that the numbers of women involved in home-based childcare work is likely to exceed the numbers of women involved in all other types of home-based work combined. The growing participation of women in the formal economy, the expansion of 'professional' jobs for women and the increased need for middle class households to have access to two incomes to maintain their standard of living have led to the development of interdependent relationships among professional and poor women. The development of opportunities for middle-class women in the formal sector has fuelled an expansion of jobs for poor women in the informal sector in the process reinforcing gender stereotypes about the responsibilities of both professional and poor women (Susser, 1991).

Ethnic minority women often end up disproportionately undertaking childcare and domestic work in the informal economy. Dallalfar (1994) describes how Iranian business women in Los Angeles who are married and have children hire co-ethnic women to carry out their domestic and childcare responsibilities while they are away from home. In this way, these entrepreneurial women create jobs for Iranian women who for a variety of reasons from lack of language skills and low educational background to not being able to work full-time cannot find employment in the formal labour market.

Romaniszyn (1996) outlines how female Polish undocumented workers end up in domestic work. While these workers are in competition with legally employed Filipino and Greek women, their undocumented status enhances employers' control over their labour and enables them to be paid substantially less than legally employed domestics. Andall (1992) argues that the growing equality of women in Italian society was a major factor in opening opportunities for women from developing societies to obtain domestic employment in Italy. As Italian women began to assert themselves in the public sphere, they created a space in the private sphere to be filled by migrant women. While the majority of women obtain legal contracts as domestic servants, a significant number fail to obtain such contracts. Andall quotes one survey which indicated that about one quarter of domestic servants in Italy were working illegally. This leaves these women migrants in an extremely precarious position. The threat of repatriation can be used by employers to gain acquiescence. Illegal domestics are often expected to work around the clock. Sexual harassment is another problem that some domestics have to deal with. The likelihood of loss of employment and ultimately the right to stay in the country may make informally employed domestics powerless in situations of sexual harassments concerning their employers.

Similar observations apply to the incorporation of immigrant women as domestic labourers into the hidden workforce of the United States. Repak (1994) outlines how the entry of unprecedented numbers of United States born women into the formal economy created a demand for domestic servants and day care providers. In Washington, where the proportion of women entering the labour force was the nation's highest at 69 per cent, demand outstripped the available provision of day care services and United States born women had to turn to alternative sources of potential childcare. This vacuum was filled by Central American women immigrants to Washington.

The effects of the abundance of new employment opportunities for indigenous American women on demand for female migrant labour is also outlined by Cornelius (1992). His research outlines how the incorporation of Californian women into the formal labour market created a booming market for undocumented female Mexican labour to provide childcare, clean houses and iron clothes. Newly arrived female Mexican migrants often found cleaning work by going from door to door and this was particularly prevalent in border cities such as San Diego, El Paso and Texas. Hence in both these cases, the availability of a cheap immigrant and often undocumented labour force enabled United States born women to enter the public sphere by passing their responsibilities within the private sphere on to the shoulders of other women.

A major report on the informal economy in Europe (Barthelemy *et al.*, 1990) carried out by the Commission of European communities indicated a further diverse range of circumstances in which women engage in informal economic activities. While the authors point out that the informal economy comprises a heterogeneous group of activities which are often region specific, nonetheless some common patterns shape women's experiences of the informal economy. The extensive use of unpaid female labour in agriculture, for example, characterizes most of the economies of southern Europe. Women were invisible, unpaid family helpers in a host of other family run businesses. Women were also predominately found in the declining and crisis ridden branches of industry and in low-status, low-paid precarious employment in the service sector. Hence, in many respects, the informal economy reinforced strong sexual division of roles and the inferior status of women (Hoyman, 1987).

CONCLUSION

Since the societal framework of individual countries is likely to differ given diverse historical and institutional developments in different states, then the feminization of non-standard employment is likely to vary from one country to another (Rubery, 1988). Hence the various examples outlined thus far may mask significant differences in the nature and extent of women's participation in informal employment in individual countries. Nonetheless, informal employment strategies which draw mainly on the low-paid and precarious labour of women seem an integral feature of all economies of Europe and the United States. A number of common themes characterize the incorporation of women into a restructured labour market.

The first is the segmented nature of both the formal and informal economy throughout Europe and the United States. This means that men and women are brought into the labour market in gender specific ways. Women predominate in education, clerical, catering, cleaning and hairdressing. Men, on the other hand, make up a disproportionate number of those in science, engineering, manufacturing, construction and transport. The tendency for women to work part-time rather than full-time further reinforces the segmented nature of the labour market as many occupations commonly seen as typically suited to women workers are offered on a part-time rather than full-time basis.

The second concerns the way in which the labour market and family sphere interrelate to produce a specifically gendered workforce. The subordination of women in the family leads to their subordination in the labour market. Women often have fragmented work careers structuring their employment around their continuing domestic responsibilities (Cousins, 1994). This impedes their chances of career success. Family ties often prohibit their geographical mobility and this acts as a further restraint on their ability to have successful careers. While of course these barriers are gradually being dismantled as more and more women adjust their family lives around career demands or forego family relationships to pursue career paths, nonetheless, it is still the case that compared to men, women are paid less, have less chance of promotion, are more likely to be found in unskilled service jobs and still tend to combine paid work with unpaid domestic work. As Davies and Rosser (1987) put it, 'the pathway to a successful career continues to be lined with patriarchal bricks'.

The third is the survival of the traditional sexual division of labour within the home and the gendered impact this has on women's opportunities for paid employment both within and outside the home. Allen (1989) argues that the sexual division of labour is not merely a division between male breadwinners and female housewives but an important ideological force. Women's unpaid work within the household and the relative freedom of men from such work results in women and men being integrated into the system of production in profoundly unequal ways. The sexual division of labour requires women to combine their productive role with their reproductive role as wife, mother and homemaker. The care of children shapes and determines the extent to which women can engage in paid employment and, as the chapter illustrated, makes women more likely to engage in paid employment from within the home. Homeworking is often regarded as an ideal option for women enabling them to merge their productive and reproductive roles by working at their own convenience, saving time and energy commuting to and from other work sites and avoiding social sanctions against going out of the home. Lim (1983) found that employers evoked the ideology of women's dependence on male primary breadwinners in order to justify the low pay and irregularity of homework. This ideology remained intact despite the women's important contributions to the family budget and the economic necessity that motivated them to participate in homeworking in the first place. This traps women in low-pay, low-status, labour intensive and often dangerous work at home and keeps intact ideological notions of women as primary carers and secondary workers.

The fourth is the resilience of patriarchal ideologies which are often sustained not only by men and employers but by women themselves. The organization and nature of work is often seen as the outcome of compromises between capital and labour. Such an approach under-estimates the extent to which women are influenced by patriarchal attitudes within the home and workplace. A number of the case studies reviewed in this chapter suggest that many women were reluctant to work outside the home due to pressure from their husbands or because of their own perceptions about their proper role in society. Hadjicostandi (1990) found that the perceived primacy of familial responsibility and the cultural construction of feminine roles coaxed many women into accepting homework as a form of employment which could be organized 'conveniently' around their household chores. Hence, the structure of the labour market and ideologies surrounding domesticity combine to limit the options available to women as a group. Flexibility has often been achieved through the conscious manipulation of the sexual division of labour. The economic success and ability of small businesses to accumulate capital is often dependent on having access to cheap female labour. In many immigrant family businesses, this labour may be unpaid and the appropriation of women's labour in this way is often justified through domestic bonds of kinship and patriarchy (Dallafar, 1994). While these factors may have different impacts on women in individual countries nonetheless it is important to emphasize the commonalities of women as wives, mothers, unpaid and paid workers in order to highlight the specific ways in which they are drawn into the informal economy throughout Europe and the United States.

7 Alienation versus Liberation: The Impact of the Informal Economy

The informal economy means all things to all people. The competing definitions of the concept outlined in Chapter 2 have led to a host of contradictory claims as to the potential of the informal economy to provide a more fulfilling work experience or dilute the inequalities of the formal economy. The world recession, the crisis of unemployment, shorter working hours and the rise in more precarious types of formal employment led to a flourishing interest in the informal economy from the 1970s onwards, as a panacea for the problems inherent in modern capitalist societies. For positive forecasters, the informal economy could function as an alternative or rival to the formal economy, provide liberation from the drudgery of alienating formal employment, act as a saviour for the unemployed or emerge as a seedbed for the development of entrepreneurship or new ways of working characterized by creativity and conviviality. For negative forecasters, the informal economy is liable to mirror the distortions and inequalities of the formal economy. Its relationship with the formal economy is likely to be parasitic and advanced capitalist societies could end up displaying the features of the dual economies encountered in the developing world separated into formal and informal sectors with the relationship between the two based on dependency and exploitation. By examining some of informal employment and work activities outlined thus far, this chapter evaluates these claims and assesses the potential impact on participants.

FORDISM VERSUS FLEXIBLE SPECIALIZATION

Work not only produces wealth, it also has a fundamental influence on our social consciousness (Windebank, 1991: 12). However, since work is often routine, oppressive and stultifying, then it can have a negative rather than positive impact on social consciousness

(Sayers, 1988). Rather than finding fulfilment and self-realization through work, people experience alienation and isolation. The Fordist system of production with its emphasis on a distinct division of labour was considered by some researchers to promote high levels of alienation. Chinoy's (1955) study of car assembly workers in post-war America illustrates the detailed division of labour associated with Fordism and its subsequent dehumanizing consequences on the workforce. Workers focus on material rewards and the consumer products their wages can be exchanged for. Their link to their work becomes highly instrumental and their ability to buy the mass consumer products emanating from Fordism compensates for the lack of job satisfaction they gain from their employment. These views are backed up by Blauner (1964) who, from a study of four different types of organization, considered assembly line workers as experiencing the highest levels of alienation. While these studies were criticized for their inherent technological determinism and their inability to look at the strategies implemented by workers to reduce alienation (see for example Beynon, 1975), nonetheless the decline in Fordism as a method of production and movement towards flexible specialization was considered as providing possibilities for more fulfilling work experiences.

In Blauner's (1964) study of four organizational forms of employment, craft workers experienced low levels of alienation due to their ability to directly control much of the work process. However, Blauner's study of craft industries was carried out during the affluent post-war period when craft industries were backed by powerful unions and workers lived in occupationally integrating communities. The revival of the craft production techniques based on flexible specialization which has characterized many regions of the developed world since the 1970s has flourished in an era of worldwide recession, international competition and massive levels of unemployment. As such, the ability of craft industrial workers to gain a high level of autonomy, job satisfaction and good working conditions is highly questionable.

Nonetheless, there is a common sense notion that working in small-scale establishments as opposed to large-scale, faceless organizations provides a more satisfying work environment. Szelenyi (1981) suggests that the restructuring of advanced industrial societies, particularly the movement to flexible specialization, carries with it the liberating potential of escape from the alienating experience of mass production. Flexible specialization fulfils the individual's search for creative alternatives. However, whether one experiences flexible specialization as a liberating or alienating experience depends on the circumstances under which individuals are drawn into flexible specialization. For highly skilled, specialist workers, the ability to channel creativity through engagement in small scale customized production is likely to be a rewarding experience. This is of course partly dependent on the control workers have over their labour and the products of their labour. Where such control is high, the level of alienation is likely to be low. However, one of the primary aims of flexible specialization is to maintain competitiveness while simultaneously reducing labour costs and one way this is achieved is by bringing workers into the labour market in informal ways. While some of these workers may be highly skilled, other structural disadvantages such as their age, gender and ethnic background may prevent them gaining suitable outlets for their creativity in the formal sector and the ability of the informal economy to compensate for the imperfections of the formal sector seems highly improbable.

As Chapter 4 illustrated, the informal economy tends to draw certain groups such as children, women and ethnic minorities into its clutches. This does not mean that these groups have unlimited access to informal employment opportunities. Rather the informal economy is beset by internal inequalities and abuses. In many instances, the informal economy operates as a 'closed shop' drawing on and exploiting the personal relationships and networks of existing informal workers. This in turn often curbs the freedom of subsequent informal workers to experience these sources of employment as liberating as they not only are indebted to their employer but also to the friendship and other networks which facilitated their entrance. This can be illustrated by briefly considering the recruitment strategies of informal employers to gain access to additional informal employees.

INFORMAL RECRUITMENT STRATEGIES

Small-scale enterprises, particularly subcontractors seeking to secure a contract, usually offer only short-term employment. They are thus less likely than large-scale enterprises to seek labour through formal channels (Morris, 1985). This is partly to do with the costs attached to formal recruitment. The more temporary the work offered, the more important it will be to minimize costs. If subcontractors intend to cut costs through the employment of informal wage labour then it is obvious that they need to minimize the risks of detection. One way they may achieve this is to utilize informal recruitment procedures. The local community is a key area where workers and management develop perceptions of the labour market. Whipp (1985) discusses historical and contemporary research which indicates how kinship and community connections are vital to employers as recruitment devices. Harris (1987) and Morris (1984) focus on the importance of social networks in enabling certain groups to gain access to informal employment. Both authors illustrate the prevalence of preferential recruitment through informal channels. Grieco (1987) refers to these informal influences as 'grapevine recruitment'. She describes how networks can be manipulated to fill local labour market vacancies.

This leads Sassen (1996) to suggest that the restructuring of the labour market has led to a shift of labour market functions to the household or community. As the need for informal workers grows, the onus is placed on current informal employees to bring in other members of their families or communities. Hence, traditional labour market functions such as recruitment, screening and training are passed from the labour market on to the household or community. In this way, the responsibilities of informal workers are enhanced. While such an tactic can be viewed as transferring control of the recruitment process to employees or communities, nonetheless, the practice also demonstrates the inherently unequal nature of the informal economy. It indicates that individuals and communities not connected to these informal networks may find it very difficult to gain access to informal employment.

Informal recruitment may also operate to the advantage of employers by facilitating the creation of low cost, exploitative employment. As Roberts (1994:17) points out, 'Local networks are important in obtaining work, whether in the informal or the formal sector, but I suspect that they serve as much to facilitate economic exploitation as economic independence'.

Informal recruits brought into the labour market via these networks may feel obligated and grateful to the person responsible for their recruitment and this may place limits on their ability to develop an objective perception of their working conditions and prospects. Workers' resistance can to some extent be controlled by peer group pressure. Indeed, the manipulation of the recruitment process through the development of these informal networks is likely to enhance the loyalty, docility, dependence and self-discipline of the workforce. On the other hand, much of the research into the alienating aspects of mass production has focused on workers' instrumental orientation to their employment and how the lack of social relationships within work enhances their alienation (see Goldthorpe *et al.*'s classic study: 1968). While these workers were compensated by high wages, informal wage labourers may have to endure a different set of alienating work conditions along with low, exploitative wage rates. Nevertheless, the personal relationships which permeate the workplace may reduce this alienation. My own research among contract cleaners in Belfast (Leonard, 1992), indicated that while the contract cleaners could be seen as being exploited by employers, their strong supportive employment networks based on kinship, friendship and neighbourhood relationships allowed the women to adopt their own labour market solutions to their economic marginalization. These networks humanized the employment experience and their refusal to be alienated from personal values could be viewed as a form of potential power.

MOONLIGHTING AS A FORM OF REWARDING EMPLOYMENT

Some commentators on the informal economy suggest that excessive state regulation and interference generates informal economic activity. De Grazia (1984) outlines the views of American, French and Italian economists and sociologists on the positive impact of moonlighting. These studies suggest that moonlighting enables individuals to circumvent government restrictions on personal initiative and provides an important barrier against excessive state interference. Wenig (1990a) argues that individuals engage in this type of informal activity to avoid being controlled. Being able to get around the rules of the system indicates the vitality of citizens and not being controlled is a positive value in itself. If moonlighters are taxed too excessively on their additional income, then this acts as a major disincentive against engaging in supplementary economic activity. Moonlighters often test out new ideas and skills in their secondary occupation to see how the market responds and if successful, transfer their resources and energy towards the full time pursuit of their once supplementary occupation. Hence moonlighting may lead to the development of formal enterprises.

Of course the economic incentive of additional income may not be the only reason for engaging in moonlighting. DeGrazia (1984) suggests that some people may engage in moonlighting because they are bored with their normal occupation and see moonlighting as a way of achieving a sense of self-satisfaction. Their talents and abilities may not be stretched enough in their main occupation or they may wish to pursue a wholly different interest through their part-time occupation. Mingione (1990b) suggests that moonlighters may wish to change jobs and use moonlighting as a kind of trial apprenticeship before making the final decision to switch jobs.

However, this rosy image of the motivations to engage in moonlighting is far removed from a number of studies into the reality of moonlighting. Alden (1981) suggests that moonlighting encourages people to work excessively long hours and this could have a potentially negative effect on their health. Moreover, they may intensify the element of risk attached to their additional occupations due to being too tired to take the necessary precautions or respond in an alert way to possible risks. Cuts in the real value of wages may encourage individuals to engage in additional jobs. Hence, rather than seeking self-fulfilment, individuals may engage in moonlighting purely for financial reasons. Moreover, concentrating on moonlighting may obscure the responses of households to economic restructuring. Moonlighting highlights the strategies of individuals and their involvement in multiple occupations. Focusing on the multiple employment strategies of individuals underplays the possible multiple employment strategies of households. While recent research indicates that the numbers of women involved in moonlighting are increasing, nonetheless, there is a general consensus from research into moonlighting in a number of countries that the typical moonlighter is male, aged between 20 and 60 and likely to have a spouse and dependent children (see for example the Final Synthesis Report of the European Commission into the informal economy, Barthelemy *et al.*, 1990). Men who decide not to become involved in moonlighting may do so not because there are no additional job opportunities available but because other members of their households are engaged in a range of formal and informal wage labour and self-provisioning activities which dilutes the necessity of their involvement in additional wage labour. In the absence of available research, these comments remain speculative but they do indicate that relying on the motivations of individuals for participating in informal economic strategies may simplify and obscure how their behaviour is shaped by wider social obligations.

THE INFORMAL ECONOMY AS A PANACEA FOR UNEMPLOYMENT

Mass unemployment has seemingly become a feature of the major economies of the western world. The spectre of unemployment has created interest in the informal economy as a way of absorbing the labour no longer needed by the formal economy. Blair (1982) outlines the importance of the informal economy for peripheral groups in the American labour market such as the unemployed. He suggests that the informal economy provides an important safety net for those people who cannot obtain jobs in the formal economy. These groups will be attracted to low-paying, off-the-books jobs in the informal economy and the availability of these jobs will provide an important safety valve function to dislocations in the formal economy.

According to this approach, the informal economy has the potential to provide practical solutions to the scourge of unemployment which has plagued developed economies by enabling formally inactive individuals to become integrated into mainstream society through involvement in informal employment. However, this positive approach, emphasizing the ability of informal economy to absorb the ranks of the unemployed, contradicts much of the research in Europe and the US which indicates that the unemployed are the group least likely to become involved in the informal economy. This is not just due to fears over possible loss of welfare benefits if detected but to very limited opportunities and social contacts. The unemployed have been portrayed as isolated and fatalistically resigned to their unemployment status in a number of studies. Yet, the numeric unimportance of the working unemployed in estimates of the extent and nature of informal work ignores the resourcefulness of those unemployed individuals who do manage to gain access to some type of informal employment. It is to this group that we now turn.

In general, accounts of the informal employment opportunities available to the unemployed have emphasized the insecurity, hard work, long and often unsociable hours, exploitative wage rates and sometimes dangerous conditions attached to this type of informal economic activity. The unemployed rarely 'choose' to become involved in informal employment preferring the security of formal employment. However, lack of formal job opportunities coupled with an inability to meet households needs in the absence of welfare benefits or because of the inadequacy of the assistance available encourages some individuals to turn to informal employment as way of actively responding to their insecure economic situation. MacDonald (1994) sees the informal employment strategies of the unemployed as part of a survival strategy through which some individuals are able to develop alternative ways of working in the face of restricted opportunities and the failure of a system of welfare benefits to adequately meet their material needs. Although the employment opportunities that are available are often temporary and sporadic, nonetheless, the ability of the unemployed to gain such work demonstrates their capabilities in successfully 'seeking out work' (Bryson and Jacobs, 1992). This approach dilutes stereotypical images of the unemployed as passive, workshy individuals content to survive on welfare handouts.

The sample of working unemployed that MacDonald's research focused on held a high commitment to upholding the values of family life through self-reliant economic behaviour and informal employment enabled them to achieve some measure of positive self-worth. Informal employment opportunities enabled the unemployed to maintain a sense of pride in themselves. Hence, rather than responding passively to the limited formal employment opportunities that were available, the unemployed in MacDonald's study were resourceful and ingenious in their attempts to secure informal employment. In this way, working while claiming benefits could be viewed as representing a culture of enterprise rather than dependency. By working informally, the unemployed demonstrated high levels of personal motivation, initiative and risk-taking (MacDonald, 1994:528).

Wenig (1990a) makes similar observations in relation to the working unemployed in Germany. He argues that by working informally the unemployed can prove to themselves and to others that they still have a valuable contribution to make to society although since often such employment has to remain hidden to avoid detection, its ability to actively demonstrate the contribution of the unemployed to the economy is highly questionable. Nonetheless,

Sheenan and Tomlinson (1996) found that while many employers viewed the long-term unemployed in extremely negative terms, these opinions were diminished if and when applicants revealed that they had been working informally as this was regarded by employers as showing motivation and initiative. While these studies justly restore powers of agency to the unemployed, we need to be cautious not to over emphasize the positive aspects of this type of informal employment.

The fact that small numbers of the unemployed are able to find some type of informal employment has often been blown out of all proportion by wildly inflated anecdotal estimates on the prevalence of this type of informal practice. These estimates have been utilized as justification for introducing stricter criteria for claiming welfare benefits or for reducing or curbing the introduction of such benefits on the basis that they are not really needed. The availability of limited informal employment opportunities for the unemployed is often utilized to avert attention away from the structural reasons for growing unemployment and from the need to tackle unemployment as a major issue. Informal employment opportunities may also dilute the critical awareness of the unemployed to seek ways to change or improve their situation. Ditton and Brown (1981:521) for example argue that 'the invisible income individuals receive from their part in the hidden economy creates subjective feelings of fantasy equality while simultaneously exacerbating real objective inequality'. They conclude that this type of informal employment supports rather than undermines the status quo. Hence, while a number of recent researchers have sought to restore powers of agency to the unemployed by seeking to highlight the ways in which they react actively rather than passively to wider structural constraints, ironically, these responses may keep intact employment strategies which exploit the circumstances some individuals find themselves in.

WOMEN AND THE INFORMAL ECONOMY

In Chapter 6, I indicated that barriers to women's participation in the formal economy often creates the conditions for their involvement in informal economic activity. However, this begs the question – do women actively choose to become involved in informal employment or do they become involved out of necessity rather than choice? Lenz and Myerhoff (1985) see the informal economy as representing an alternative value system. Some of the opportunities available to women in the informal economy allow them to reduce the conflict between work and household life and hence humanize the employment experience. Clearly, if Lenz and Myerhoff are right, homeworking should provide women with such an opportunity. It is to an examination of homeworking as an active strategy implemented by women to merge the demands of home and employment that we now turn.

Homeworking is often viewed as a strategy implemented by employers to gain access to a cheap, flexible labour force. A number of the studies outlined in Chapter 6 back up this observation by highlighting the often exploitative conditions associated with homeworking. In these studies, homeworking is seen as an option imposed on women in the absence of viable alternatives. However, recent researchers into homeworking have challenged this notion of women passively responding to external structural constraints. Dangler (1994) argues that homeworking is not simply the result of an imposition by employers seeking access to cheap labour but the result of women's efforts to find income-earning opportunities in highly restricted circumstances. Rising male unemployment, cuts in welfare provisions, low formal employment opportunities, husbands' resistance to wives·employment outside the household, the survival of the traditional gendered division of labour in the household and the absence of low-cost childcare all converge to make homeworking an option for women. While exploitative conditions remain an inevitable feature of most types of homework, nonetheless, Dangler argues that women homeworkers can be regarded as taking a sense of control over the structural disadvantages they face in the wider society. The homeworkers interviewed by Dangler expressed preferences for homework over the boring, repetitive jobs many of them had previously engaged in outside the household.

While for many women the decision to engage in homework was illusory in that there were few viable alternatives, nonetheless, the efforts of women to cope with and dilute wider structural constraints is often absent from many studies of homeworking. Costello (1988) found that homework earnings had a positive effect on women's input into family decision making. With the earnings gained from homeworking, some women became more assertive in relation to their husbands. Homeworking provided other women with opportunities to become small-scale entrepreneurs. Highlighting these more positive features of homeworking should not detract attention away from the often exploitative features of homeworking but they do suggest a more complex relationship between employers' strategies and workers' needs. While homeworking does provide employers with opportunities to gain access to a flexible workforce, it only does so because it combines with women's initiatives to carve out practical work options given the limitations imposed on them by the wider society. While the long-term efforts of feminism should be to remove these wider constraints, in the short term homeworking does provide some women with the opportunity to respond actively to the constraints imposed on their ability to seek employment outside the household.

COLLECTIVE RESPONSES, SURVIVAL STRATEGIES AND THE INFORMAL ECONOMY

The responses of households and communities to restructuring through involvement in informal economic activities have often been referred to as 'survival strategies'. The words to some extent contradict one another. The term strategy indicates some sort of plan involving an element of choice while the word survival indicates circumstances in which alternative choices are likely to be limited. The initial usage of this term was restricted to developing societies where the poor in the shanty towns that accompanied the growth of 'third world' cities seemed able to eke out an existence in the absence of formal employment opportunities and a welfare state. However, as more and more studies of the prevalence of the informal economy in the cities of the developed world take place, the term is utilized to refer to the coping strategies of groups marginalized in the formal economy. Nonetheless, while the informal economy may provide opportunities for those disadvantaged in the formal economy, it is important to go beyond seeing the informal economy as merely a coping strategy of the poor. Such an approach may lead to the mistaken view that the informal economy is marginal to the formal economy. This neglects the myriad of ways in which the two sectors are interconnected. Benton (1990) for example, found that small-scale sweatshops and homeworkers in Spain were linked to subcontracting chains that transcended national boundaries. Sassen (1991) found that the urban middle class in American cities consumed a substantial amount of the products and services of the informal economy. These examples indicate that the informal economy constitutes an integral part of the overall economy.

The connections between the formal and informal economy are also apparent in the responses of local communities to economic restructuring. Rather than simply operating as a survival strategy, the existence of community networks can sometimes promote community growth and enhance the chances of marginalized individuals to transfer their activities to the formal sector. Stepick (1990) illustrates this by examining the importance of informal community networks for Cubans compared to Haitians in Miami. The US government discouraged the migration of Haitians to the United States and this negative attitude affected the subsequent treatment of Haitians in the labour force and contributed to their marginalization in the formal and informal economy. While some Haitians ended up as informal entrepreneurs, Stepick points out that this was a last resort strategy. Haitians preferred the security of wage labour to the insecurity which characterized their involvement in self-employment. These entrepreneurs served almost exclusively a low-income Haitian market which provided almost no opportunities for self advancement. While Haitians became concentrated in specific geographical areas, these provided little illustration of thriving community networks. Goods and services did flow among community members but did little to dilute the collective isolation of Haitians from the broader economy.

Miami's Cuban enclave by contrast was vibrant and provided new migrants with strong possibilities for self-advancement. Unlike Haitians, Cubans were welcomed by the US government and benefitted from various forms of support for refugees. This enabled some Cubans to quickly become entrepreneurs and the availability of a large, low-wage informal Cuban labour force greatly contributed to the success of these initial entrepreneurs. Cubans voluntarily submitted to exploitative forms of wage labour for fellow Cubans on the understanding that they might receive future support to develop their own businesses. In this way, the informal practices of the Cuban community created a vital dynamic sector which enabled Cubans to experience rapid socio-economic advancement sometimes at the expense of other immigrant groups. Gradually some of these informal ventures became integrated into the formal economy. However, while this success story does indicate the potential importance of collective networks in facilitating the transfer of resources to internal community members nonetheless such networks need to be accompanied by favourable state policies to ensure that the needs of marginal groups are met.

Intra-household exchanges of goods and services have been viewed as reducing the dependence of communities on external bodies such as the state and fostering and developing autonomous community development. However, the political rhetoric of support for self-help which surrounds these notions of community needs to be placed in the wider context of Rightist policies justifying the retreat of the state in a number of European countries and the US (Redclift and Mingione, 1985). Godard (1985) argues that there is a tendency in some sociological studies to suggest that mutual aid within community networks is preferable to the external services provided by the welfare state. By reducing reliance on collective state services, individuals experience empowerment and needs are more effectively met through the personal touch of friends, neighbours and relatives. This approach thus suggests a familistic solution to the crisis of the welfare state. However, a report into informal care in Europe (Twigg, 1993) indicates that responsibility for such care falls disproportionately on women's shoulders and rather than empowering women entrenches normative expectations surrounding women's roles as mothers, housewives and natural carers.

Moreover, as Chapter 5 indicated, intra-household co-operation was often based on the principle of reciprocity. Hence the needs of those unable to reciprocate were left unmet. This again illustrates the inherent inequalities of the informal sector. Rather than a panacea for the failures of the formal system, the informal economy often further marginalizes those rejected by the formal economy. It seems unlikely that community networks can be utilized effectively to play any great part in the care of non relatives or those unable to reciprocate. Friends and neighbours tend to provide banal, mundane favours that enable others to cope with the haphazard contingencies they face rather than provide a consistent source of long-term effective support (Leonard, 1997; Morris, 1994).

Leira (1993) argues that the supposed existence of such networks nonetheless prevents welfare states from facing a legitimation crisis that their policies in dismantling welfare systems' might otherwise provoke. In this way, these networks, however ineffective, act as a safety valve rather than a challenge to the status quo. Henry (1982) suggests that a major weakness of informal economies is that they mask the failures of the formal economy. Hence, while the existence of such networks may provide some individuals with access to otherwise unobtainable goods and services, 'in doing so, they effectively palliate those with immediate needs and pacify the most vociferous of society's critics who are deluded into thinking their problems are solvable through local action' (Henry, 1982:22). It is clear that some types of informal economic activity are not simply solutions to individual subsistence problems or household or community needs. Rather, informal economic activity is often bound up in the failures of states to provide citizens with a decent standard of living. As Weiss (1987:231) states, it is frequently the need to circumvent the inadequacies of the state that throws citizens back on informal support systems. Hence, rather than displacing the need for informal networks, the very organization of modern welfare states sustains and enlarges the operation of such networks.

THE INFORMAL ECONOMY AND THE ISSUE OF CHOICE

The issue of choice is central to any evaluation of the positive or negative benefits of involvement in informal economic strategies. If individuals are forced into informal economic activities out of lack of viable alternatives, then the potential for such activities to empower individuals seems slim. One could argue that involvement in the informal economy could heighten individuals' awareness of the deficiencies of the system, however a number of the studies referred to earlier seem to indicate that involvement in the informal economy acts as a safety value rather than a challenge to the status quo. Sometimes, as Dangler's (1994) study of homeworkers points out, the needs of employers can coincide with the needs of workers for non-standard forms of employment. Yet, while it is refreshing to see a perspective that focuses on women as active economic agents in the face of limited opportunities, it remains difficult to view such work as potentially liberating for the women involved. Pinnaro and Pugliese (1985) in an interesting study of the informal economy in Naples suggested that some individuals, despite their precarious economic situation, resisted entry to the informal economy because they simply found its conditions too unattractive. However this decision to defy the opportunities for participation in informal employment was more open to young adult males and less open to women and children. This indicates that involvement in the informal economy may be less liberating than resisting or escaping from the reach of the informal economy. It is unfortunate that for some groups of individuals, the decision of whether or not to engage in informal economic activity is an illusory one.

INFORMAL WORKERS: WITH OR WITHOUT CHAINS

It is difficult to reach a satisfactory conclusion as to the potential of the informal economy to provide individuals with a more satisfactory, inherently rewarding form of economic activity. Often, research on the informal economy is concerned more with estimating its extent and significant than with establishing the motives of actors to engage in informal work and employment. The qualitative studies that are available often concentrate on sub-samples of participants in the informal economy and do not pay enough attention to comparisons between those who decide to engage in informal economic activity and those who do not, despite seemingly similar circumstances. While the informal economy may provide a source of self-fulfilment and opportunities for upward mobility for some groups, it is clear that these effects are very uneven and less likely for groups such as the unemployed, women, children and ethnic minorities. On the other hand, this generalization is easy to disprove. Some of the unemployed have been able to utilize the informal economy as a way of gaining access to more secure, formal employment. Some women have been able to utilize involvement in the informal economy as a means of starting a business in the formal economy or have managed to respond positively to ideological constraints which operate against them taking up employment outside the home by engaging in income earning activities within the household. While it is easy to dismiss such responses as doing little to challenge stereotypical notions of women's natural roles in society, nonetheless, such practices enabled some women to enhance their bargaining power within the household. Not all ethnic groups were marginalized by the informal economy. In some cases, ethnic groups were able to collectively benefit from access to informal employment and utilize such opportunities to develop niches for economic advancement in the formal economy. These examples indicate the diverse nature of the impact of the informal economy on its varied participants. While it seems unrealistic to consider informal workers as 'workers without chains' (Pahl, 1980:17), nonetheless it is equally unrealistic to dismiss such activities as marginal and unimportant. Through involvement in a whole range of informal work and employment practices, individuals, households and communities can and do make choices and some of the decisions they make enable them to respond actively to the social and economic constraints which they face.

8 Conclusions

In the context of global stagnation and economic crises, increased competition and the internationalization of the division of labour, employers and workers have turned to informal economic activities in attempts to achieve some level of economic security in a highly precarious environment. Decentralization has become a key strategy in the restructuring of global capital leading to the proliferation of new and atypical forms of employment. Temporary jobs, substitutions, piecework, homework and subcontracting are part of this general trend. This book attempts to examine the impact of these changes in Europe and the United States. Of course, similar economic trends do not have similar consequences. In order to try to make sense of the overall framework in which the informal economy is situated, broad, general processes have been highlighted at the expense of local, regional and national differences. Global restructuring often has regionally specific impacts and different regional manifestations. However, it is clear that these changes are producing increasingly 'untidy patterns of work and employment' (Pahl, 1990) and it is to these messy forms of economic activity that the book is addressed.

In Chapter 2, I suggested that the meaning of what is formal/informal, regular/irregular, registered/unregistered varies within and across countries. This makes it very difficult to provide a comprehensive definition of what constitutes informal economic activity. The most common approach is to define the informal economy as all economic activity excluding criminal activity that is not recorded in national accounts. This definition is adopted in the book but extended to include productive activities in households and communities, as well as the unreported and unrecorded economic activity associated with tax evasion and benefit fraud. However, given the scope of countries under consideration here, any attempt to provide a universal definition is fraught with difficulties. Since states have different fiscal policies, what is considered tax evasion in one country may be perfectly legal in another. States also have different levels of welfare provision. Hence activities which are morally condemned in states with sophisticated welfare policies or influenced by new right ideologies may be embraced by states with low levels of provision as a way of diluting the failures of the formal system.

To some extent then the state creates the informal economy by virtue of its role in regulating economic activity. The ways in which economic activities are counted and regulated are a vital element of state revenues. Non payment of taxes and social security contributions aggravates the difficulties of financing the public debt and subsidizing the cost of social security systems. Throughout the twentieth century, the state has also played an active role in ensuring the collective well-being of the workforce. The state is therefore involved in regulating the relations between capital and labour and the conditions under which work is performed. Informal economic activities may be prompted by the desire to evade health, safety and employment regulations rather than simply avoid tax payments.

However, state activity itself is subject to historical and cultural variation (Lozano, 1989). Hence, in some countries, the state may take an active role in attempting to regulate informal economic activity while in other countries, states may foster informal employment in order to dilute the negative side effects of unemployment and other economic crises. Moreover, national state policy may have local and regional effects. A number of studies on the informal economy in Italy for example, emphasize the role of regional rather than national politics in determining the nature and scope of informal economic activity. These variant political processes have enabled the informal economy to develop as a source of upward mobility in some regions while existing as little more than a survival mechanism in others. The socio-political priorities of the state are therefore shaped by local political actors, the availability and willingness of the labour force to become involved in informal economic activities and the requirements of employers for labour that can be employed under a variety of arrangements. Hence, the state by itself is not responsible for the informal economy but plays an important role in structuring its existence.

These themes were developed in Chapter 3 which briefly examined the historical development of the distinctions which emerged between work and employment in a number of countries. Industrialization led to a clear separation between the private world and work of the household and the public world of formal paid employment. The latter was elevated as the purest form of work and other forms of work which existed outside this limited definition were rendered invisible and considered economically unimportant.

The concept of Fordism was utilized to describe the system of mass production and mass consumption which characterized the post-war period up until the global recession of the early 1970s. This was not meant to imply that Fordism was the only or indeed even the dominant model of production available. Altshuler (1985) argues that Fordism was not simply *adopted* outside of North America but significantly *adapted*. Hence it is difficult to ascertain whether seemingly similar production processes were extensions of Fordism or a movement beyond it.

My intention here was to utilize Fordism as an ideal type to demonstrate its impact on the development of a classic model of employment based on lifetime employment with a single company from training to retirement. Such a model of employment based on guarantees of the right to work backed by welfare provision to overcome temporary setbacks dominated the affluent post-war economic stability which characterized the US and much of Northern Europe. Southern Europe by contrast continued to display features of what might be termed pre-Fordism or peripheral Fordism characterized by sporadic, more diverse working arrangements.

The stable economic position of the US and Europe was shaken by the growing instability which typified the 1970s. In a context of intense global competition and uncertainty, decentralization arose as a key strategy on the part of capital to cheapen and re-establish control over the labour force. Flexible specialization emerged as a tactic to reduce the risks imposed by economic uncertainty. Industrial activity became increasingly characterized by vertical disintegration. Multi-national corporations subcontract to local firms who subcontract to middlemen who further subcontract to petty commodity producers or homeworkers. The decentralization of activities through subcontracting has developed as a key economic strategy in the transformation of core economies from manufacturing-based to service-based economies. De-industrialization in the United States, the Federal Republic of Germany, France, Italy and Britain has been marked by a shift from manufacturing to tertiary sector activity. It is within this context that vertical disintegration allows large firms to subcontract out a range of services formally done in-house. These processes give rise to informal ways of working. New strategies of capital accumulation and economic restructuring have led to the replacement of secure, full-time employment with less regular, more atypical, non-standard forms of employment. While some of these employment practices remain in the formal sectors, others are increasingly available in the informal sector as firms seek to lower labour costs through non-payment of taxes and avoidance of other costly regulations concerning protective measures for workers.

The development of informal economic activities is not simply due to the political privilege of the state to intervene in the economy but to tendencies in the contemporary world economy to create categories of labour that are more highly exploited and less easily protected than others (Lozano, 1989). Chapter 4 highlights the ways in which children, ethnic minorities and the unemployed are drawn into informal economic activity while Chapter 6 looks at the inclusion of women in the informal economy. Emphasizing the incorporation of these groups into the informal economy does not imply that informal employment is simply a peripheral type of labour undertaken mainly by marginalized populations as a survival strategy. The case studies reviewed in the chapter, by contrast, clearly link the involvement of these groups in the informal economy to, among other things, the restructuring of capital and its tendency to create new forms of employment. Hence the groups drawn into the labour market as part of this process are central rather than marginal to the workings of advanced capitalism. The availability and vulnerability of these workers enables employers in developed countries to obtain 'cheap' labour at home rather than seek such labour in developing countries. This is especially useful for enterprises too small to shift production abroad. The presence of a flexible, indigenous, workforce willing to work for low rates of pay and often in poor conditions enables small scale firms to match the low labour costs of their developing world competitors. Mitter (1986) argues that the availability of a flexible labour force resulted in a visible shift in production through subcontracting from the developing world to western European countries throughout the 1980s. Highlighting these links indicates the intricate relationship between the formal and the informal economy. Rather than separate spheres, the book illustrates how even seemingly isolated homeworkers are often linked to subcontracting chains that connect local, national and international economies.

Chapter 4 includes a brief discussion on moonlighting. The purpose of looking at moonlighting is to highlight further linkages between the formal and informal economy by looking at workers employed in both spheres. Moonlighters shift from the formal to the informal economy thus blurring the divisions between the two. Moonlighting also involves the issue of tax evasion which is often considered the primary motivation for involvement in the informal economy. The whole thrust of the book is to demonstrate the peripheral types of work that often exist in the informal economy and the vulnerable groups that tend to become ideal recruits for informal economic practices. However, this is only one side of the story and while I would argue that it is these exploitative types of informal employment that are likely to persist given the likelihood of continuing competition, economic uncertainty and periodic recessions, nonetheless the presence of informal employment opportunities is beneficial for some workers. Moonlighters, for example, can maintain or enhance their standard of living through involvement in additional informal employment outside of their mainstream occupation. In some cases, these additional employment arrangements can provide some workers with opportunities to test new ideas and form the seedbed for future formal entrepreneurial ventures. The book includes other examples which demonstrates how some groups such as certain ethnic minorities are able to use the existence of informal employment opportunities to create niches beneficial for facilitating the upward mobility of participants and their eventual transition to the formal economic sphere.

Chapter 5 focused on the household and the community relationships in which work is embedded. Household strategies were divided into two main types. The first concerned the self-provisioning activities of multiple earner households. These practices drew on the unfinished products available in the formal market. The internal labour input of household members was utilized to transform these partially finished products into final goods and services for individual privatized household consumption. The second household strategy referred to the survival strategies implemented by poorer households to enable them to cope with economic uncertainty and fluctuating relationships to formal and informal wage labour. The chapter cautioned against seeing household strategies as consensual responses to external constraints. The literature reviewed in the chapter indicated that household solidarity may be based on coercion, self rather than collective interest and responses to lack of alternative lines of action.

Chapter 5 also investigated the extent to which local communities play an important role in assisting a household's capacity to achieve a level of economic security. The evidence presented indicate that while urban residential patterns and the instability of the nuclear family have undermined the development of community networks, nonetheless, among some low-income populations characterized by low levels of social mobility and geographical stability, community networks can play a crucial role in enabling households to respond to periods of economic insecurity. Roberts (1989) in a comparison of precarious types of wage labour in Britain, Spain and Mexico suggests that family and community relationships are vital in enabling individuals to make inadequate incomes stretch to meet their daily needs. The chapter demonstrated a variety of ways in which households and communities attempt to reduce their dependence on the market. A number of locality studies indicate how some communities are characterized by intricate exchanges of goods and services. Community relationships also provide access to information about informal job opportunities and, as Mingione (1987) points out, protect vulnerable individuals from the competitive pressures of the formal labour market. However, evidence was also presented in the chapter to suggest caution over the extent to which these community networks can compensate for the failures of the formal economy. Community exchanges are profoundly unequal and mainly rely on the principle of reciprocity inducing the isolation and neglect of those unable to participate because of their inability to reciprocate. Hence Abrams (Bulmer, 1986) warns against encouraging a return to the conditions which seem to generate 'neighbourliness' as such networks often mask highly exploitative internal inequalities.

Chapter 6 looked at women's involvement in the informal economy. The chapter outlines how conventional economic theories and analyses of labour exclude the fact that much of women's work occurs in families and households outside of the context of the regulated economy. Yet these activities are fundamental to economic life (Beechey, 1987). Recent analyses concerning gender and the informal sector have acknowledged the fundamental role of women's unwaged work in global restructuring (Smith, 1984, Mies, 1986). The chapter illustrated the potent relationships between women's unwaged household work, informal sector work and formal labour markets (Beneria and Roldan, 1987). The main thrust of the chapter was on the ways in which women, particular from ethnic minority groups, are drawn into informal economic activities in areas which reinforced stereotypical images of femininity and bolster patriarchal structures both within and outside the household. While the informal economy is often presented as providing women with ideal income-earning opportunities, these choices were often imaginary and were based on lack of viable alternatives.

Chapter 7 looked at the extent to which involvement in the informal economy might reduce alienation. To some extent, this is dependent on whether or not flexibility has equally beneficial consequences for employers and employees. Pollert (1988) suggests that discussions on the nature of flexibility in modern capitalist societies often mask the vital political concern of the different issues at stake. This leads her to ask the vital question – whose flexibility and in whose interests? The chapter sought to answer this question by examining the extent to which flexibility is simply a strategy implemented by employers to lower labour costs and increase flexibility or whether it provides workers themselves with a more attractive alternative to the rigidly structured environment of the factory or office. While the book highlights the numerous ways in which the informal economy operates as a highly exploitative sphere channelling the energies of the most vulnerable in society into productive work, nonetheless, there are instances when participants are able to utilize the informal sector as a springboard for more regular, well-paid economic activity, in some cases involving transfer to the formal sector. Sometimes the needs of employers and informal employees coincided and each benefitted to different degrees from the flexible working arrangements available. While some of the strategies implemented by vulnerable groups seem trivial, nonetheless they could be seen as forms of resistance enacted by those commonly viewed as powerless in society. Roberts (1991:138) suggests that attributing strategies to individuals, households and communities indicates that despite 'the importance of structural constraints, choice is possible and that the exercise of choice can result in alternative outcomes'.

POLICY IMPLICATIONS

There are at least three ways in which states can respond to the existence of an informal economy. Firstly, they can attempt to control informal economic activity; secondly, they can choose to ignore the informal economy and thirdly, they can attempt to legalize the informal economy. In this concluding section, these three responses are considered.

States responding to the existence of an informal sector are faced with a quandary regarding wanting to encourage entrepreneurial attitudes and self-help and wanting to reduce the potentially divisive effects of tax evasion and welfare abuse. Since it is difficult to provide accurate estimates of the scale of the informal economy, then it follows that calculations on the amount of revenue lost through tax evasion or welfare abuse are equally suspect. Large-scale corporate fraud lies outside the range activities covered in this book as the emphasis is on the types of employment and work initiatives undertaken by individuals and petty commodity producers but it seems probable that this type of monetary evasion is likely to far outstrip the potential of income tax evasion and welfare abuse to defraud the state. Changes in the tax system could weaken the incentives associated with operating in the informal economy. Contemporary tax systems in many industrial countries weigh more heavily on labour intensive activities which have low productivity, use simple technology and are executed by small firms (Skolka, 1987). This is one of the reasons why such firms are prone to tax evasion. One way to resolve this is to reduce tax rates in areas where distortions are likely to be high and increase tax rates in areas where distortions are likely to be less of a problem (Smith, 1986). High levels of taxation encourage individuals to try and bypass tax demands and this in turn could lead to inefficient firms evading tax being able to undercut their more honest and possibly more efficient competitors. This is particularly likely to be the case in an era of subcontracting where tenders are often awarded to firms who can carry out the work cheaply. Such firms may be able to submit ridiculously low tenders due to their ability to hire some of their labour force off-the-books. The incentives to produce cheap tenders and secure contracts may perpetuate the usage of exploitative types of informal employment.

In relation to welfare abuse, the general conclusions emerging from the studies reviewed here were that everywhere the unemployed are less likely to be involved in informal economic activities compared to the already employed. This is not merely due to the fear of losing benefits but to lack of opportunities and low integration into information networks concerning both formal and informal job vacancies. Where such limited opportunities exist, the financial return is generally very low. Some countries such as the UK spend a substantial amount on trying to cut down on welfare abuse despite continuing indications that the amounts reclaimed are often insignificant. Indeed, Cook (1989) found that the amount of unclaimed benefits far exceeded the amount recovered by officials investigating false claims for welfare. This was also borne out by Neef's (1992) comparison of welfare systems in Britain, France and West Germany. In all three countries, a substantial amount of welfare benefits were never claimed. The main issue here is that the resources spent on attempting to recover lost income could be more effectively spent on other areas such as job creation schemes. Wenig (1990b) suggests that the unemployed should be allowed to earn a certain amount without it affecting their welfare benefits in order to encourage the value of self-help. While some states do have these types of policy in place, the amount individuals are able to earn without it affecting benefit entitlements is so low that the informal employment practices that are declared are little more than survival strategies. Wenig suggests that if allowances were more generous then the working unemployed may be able to implement strategies that result in their transfer to formal employment.

In outlining a range of studies into tax evasion in the US and the UK, Thomas (1992) suggests that the majority of respondents feel that taxes are too high and that the tax system is unfair. These attitudes are utilized by tax evaders to justify the practice particularly in instances where small gains are made. While the studies reviewed in Chapter 4 indicate that welfare abuse is the least significant aspect of the informal economy, nonetheless, Thomas suggests that in a number of countries including the US, the UK, France and Germany, a large majority of people believe that social security abuse is widespread. This has led some states such as the UK to pursue policies aimed at controlling what is in essence a marginal aspect of the informal economy while leaving undisturbed the more serious practices of large-scale organizations.

The revenue lost through tax evasion and social security abuse may be a minor problem compared to the other pitfalls connected with the existence of an informal sector. Employers, for example, may employ labour off-the-books not just to evade tax responsibilities but to avoid the ever increasing range of legislation aimed at protecting employees' rights and security. Some firms may attempt to bypass health, safety and other regulations by transferring part or all of their activities to the informal sector. Operating unofficially also enables employers to avoid the bureaucracy involved with running a business in terms of licences and other necessary permissions needed to carry out a range of activities. However, these practices could provide the seedbed for the development of subsequent thriving formal business ventures. Hence, attempts by the state to control and regulate the presence of informal sector activities may curb the potential of these enterprises to shift to the formal sector.

Of course, some states may choose to ignore the existence of an informal sector. This is particularly likely to be the response of states in southern Europe where the informal economy may be tacitly encouraged as a necessary survival strategy because of inadequate welfare provision. Mingione (1994a) suggests that a high tolerance of tax evasion is keeping alive a large number of jobs in southern Europe which would otherwise disappear. In Greece, for example, the state welfare system is weak and undeveloped. This in turn encourages the development of irregular forms of employment and the persistence of traditional family and household working arrangements. Unpaid family work is crucial in agriculture and the tourist industry. Since 1986, the state has become aware that a substantial part of the Greek economy is beyond its control. This is fuelled by high rates of self-employment, the survival of traditional small-scale activities and complex mixes of intensive seasonal work. While the Greek government has introduced a number of measures from the mid 1980s to control aspects of the informal economy such as industrial homeworking, it recognizes the limits of state policy in this area. Hence, it has simultaneously followed a policy of ignoring features of the informal economy that it acknowledges as essential to family survival. The absence of enforceable regulations governing the labour market ensures the continuing vitality of the informal sector.

The third possible response of states' concern attempts to legalize the informal economy. This involves transferring activities from the informal to the formal sector. A number of countries, for example, throughout the 1980s have attempted to regulate rather than ban homeworking. However, Mingione (1994a) argues that while such a strategy had limited success in Germany, it was less effective in Italy and Greece where homeworkers continued to experience exploitative rates of pay and poor working conditions. Chamot (1988) argues that the shift towards lifting the ban on certain types of homeworking in the US is based on a conservative ideology of 'a woman's place is in the home'. Encouraging women to work from home reduces the need for states to provide decent affordable childcare and make adequate provisions for the sick and elderly.

Hence, in this case, attempting to bring homeworking more firmly into the ranks of the formal economy may in the process reinforce women's disproportionate responsibilities within the household.

Some states have attempted to legalize the informal economy by making participation less attractive. A number of countries have tried to achieve this through deregulation. This has involved introducing provisions to enable employers to employ labour on a more flexible, atypical basis. This reduces the incentive for companies to hide their workforce. Roberts (1989) suggests that states have followed policies to deregulate on the grounds that greater flexibility would foster more rapid economic growth. In the UK, the withdrawal of job protection or lack of enforcement of labour legislation has played a major factor in the growth of atypical forms of employment. Standing (1986) argues that weaker trade unions have enabled employers to hire people more frequently on a casual basis, reduced obligations to part-time workers and diminished protection for low-paid workers. This has led Mingione (1994a) to observe that formalization through 'pure deregulation' is likely to do little to change the working conditions of peripheral groups nor provide them with favourable economic or employment opportunities.

The US labour market is considered to be the most flexible of all developed countries. Here, precedence is given to the workings of the free market and deregulation is the norm. While the success of this model in stabilizing employment is often highlighted, Jackson (1995) suggests that such a policy encourages the unemployed to take up low paid and insecure jobs. The results of this strategy lie in the fact that the real wages of the poorest 10 per cent of workers are below the level they were at in 1970 (Jackson, 1995:5). Hence, deregulation has made American society more unequal. The UK is increasingly adopting the US model (Fletcher, 1997). This can be seen in a number of recent policy initiatives. The Job Seekers Allowance introduced in October 1996 and the American-style Working Families Tax Credit introduced in March 1998 represent ways of encouraging the unemployed to take up the low-paid and precarious jobs which a deregulated labour market is increasingly creating (Finn, 1996). In 1998, France also introduced a 'welfare to work' programme modelled explicitly on the US and UK. Part of this strategy involves paying employment subsidies to employers to encourage them to recruit the long-term unemployed. From June 1998, the British government's 'passport to work' scheme involves paying employers a £75 per week subsidy for employing anyone who has been unemployed for two years or more. The effects of this scheme remain to be seen. Other European countries such as Belgium, Germany, Portugal, Ireland and Greece have extensive programmes of wage subsidies (Fletcher, 1997). Italy and Spain also have schemes to reduce the social security contributions of employers recruiting the long-term unemployed and similar measures were introduced in the UK in 1998. However, in the majority of these countries, employment subsidies have not been used to lower wages but rather to encourage the hiring of the long-term unemployed at existing wage rates (Finn, 1996). By contrast the US, the UK and France seem to be creating a climate where the unemployed have little option but to take up any type of work that becomes available regardless of pay levels, job prospects or durability.

This brings me to a final important point. To some extent, the focus on whether specific activities fall into the formal or the informal sector is misplaced. As we have seen, the boundaries between the formal and informal economy are continually shifting so that an activity may be defined as part of the informal economy in one period of time and part of the formal economy in another. Moreover, definitions change from one country to another as do states' responses to the informal economy. This again makes it difficult to establish universal criteria for determining what should be included as part of the informal economy. A more profitable approach is to perhaps examine more fully contemporary changes in work and employment regardless of whether such changes promote the rise of an informal economy or an extension of the formal one. It is clear that the future of employment is fraught with uncertainties. Technological advances, cyclical booms and recessions and the shrinking of the labour market through local, national and international competition encourage the development of new forms of employment along with widespread unemployment. The ways in which individuals, households and communities are influenced by and respond to these changes will differ and depend upon the relationship between the state, capital and labour not only in each country but often within specific regions within each country. While some groups may benefit from these changes, it is likely that others may find themselves in less favourable, more precarious positions. Where these changes influence the spread of unfavourable informal employment opportunities, there is a tendency for researchers to imply that if such activities were to be formalized, the potential abuse of labour associated with the informal economy would disappear or at least be significally diluted. Such an approach ignores the similarities between peripheral workers in both the formal and informal economy. Waldinger and Lapp (1993) for example suggest that the real scandal associated with the rise of sweatshops in New York is the growth in *legal* forms of employment which pay such low wages that they do not provide an adequate standard of living. Women, children and ethnic minority groups in particular will play a key role in future compromises between states, capital and labour. While some gains will be made, others will find themselves on the margins of the formal and informal economy. While, of course, trade-offs will be regionally and nationally specific, nonetheless, it is only by recognizing the commonalities between the positions of certain groups within the formal and informal economy that the forces which give rise to exploitative forms of labour can be more fully understood and challenged.

References

Alden, J. (1981) 'Holding Two Jobs: an Examination of Moonlighting' in Henry, S. (ed.) *Can I Have It In Cash*, London: Astragal Books.

Alford, R.R. and Feige, E.L. (1989) 'Information Distortions in Social Systems: the Underground Economy and other Observer-subject-policymaker Feedbacks' in Feige, E.L. (ed.) *The Underground Economies*, Cambridge: Cambridge University Press.

Allen, S. (1989) 'Locating Homework in an Analysis of the Ideological and Material Constraints on Women's Paid Work' in Boris, E. and Daniels, C. (eds.) *Homework: Historical and Contemporary Perspectives on Paid Labour at Home*, Chicago: University of Illinois Press.

Allen, S. (1996) Review of Phizacklea, A. and Wolkowitz, C. (1995), 'Homeworking Women: Gender, Racism and Class at Work', *Sociology*, Vol. 30. No. 1. pp. 192–3.

Allen, S. and Wolkowitz, C. (1987) *Homeworking: Myths and Realities*, London: Macmillan.

Altshuler, A. (1985) *The Future of the Automobile*, Cambridge: MA, MIT Press.

Andall, J. (1992) 'Women Migrant Workers in Italy', *Women's Studies International Forum*, Vol. 15. No. 1. pp. 41–8.

Bachman, J.G. and Schulenberg, J. (1993) 'How Part-Time Work Intensity Relates to Drug Use, Problem, Behaviour, Time Use and Satisfaction Among High School Seniors: Are These Consequences or Merely Correlates?', *Development Psychology*, Vol. 29. No. 2. pp. 220–35.

Bagnasco, A. (1990) 'The Informal Economy' *Current Sociology*, pp. 157–75.

Bailey, T. and Waldinger, R. (1991) 'Primary, Secondary and Enclave Labor Markets: a Training Systems Approach, *American Sociological Review*, No. 56. pp. 432–45.

Barou, J. (1987) 'In the Aftermath of Colonization: Black African Immigrants' in Buechler, H.C. and Buechler, J.M. (eds) *Migrants in Europe: the Role of Family, Labor and Politics*, Westport, Connecticut: Greenwood Press.

Barthelemy, P. (1989) 'The Underground Economy in France' in Feige, E.L. (ed.) *The Unofficial Economies*, Cambridge: Cambridge University Press.

Barthelemy, P., Miguelez, F., Mingione, E., Pahl, R. and Wenig, A. (1990) *Underground Economy and Irregular Forms of Employment, Final Synthesis Report*, Luxembourg: Commission of the European Communities.

Bawly, D. (1982) *The Subterranean Economy*, New York: McGraw-Hill.

Beechey, V. (1987) *Unequal Work*, London: Verso.

Bell, D. (1974) *The Coming of Post-Industrial Society*, London: Heinemann.

Bell, D. and Roach, B. (1989) 'Moonlighting: The Economic Reality of Teaching?', *Education*, No. 110. pp. 397–400.

Beneria, L. (1988) 'Conceptualizing the Labour Force: the Underestimation of Women's Economic Activities' in R.E. Pahl, (ed.) *On Work: Historical, Comparative and Theoretical Approaches*, Oxford: Blackwell.

Beneria, L. and Roldan, M. (1987) *The Crossroads of Class and Gender: Industrial Homework, Subcontracting and Household Dynamics in Mexico City*, Chicago: Chicago University Press.

Benton, L.A. (1989) 'Industrial Subcontracting and the Informal Sector: The Politics of Restructuring in the Madrid Electronics Industry' in Portes, A., Castello, M. and Benton, L. (eds.) *The Informal Economy: Studies in Advanced and Less Developed Countries*, Baltimore: John Hopkins University Press.

Benton, L.A. (1990) *Invisible Factories: the Informal Economy and Industrial Development in Spain*, Albany: State University of New York Press.

Beynon, H. (1975) *Working for Ford*, Wakefield: EP. Publishing.

Blades, D. (1982) 'The Hidden Economy and National Accounts', OECD Economic Outlook, *Occasional Studies*, June, pp. 28–45.

Blair, J.P. (1982) 'Irregular Economies', in Gappert, G. and Knight, R.V. (eds.) *Cities in the 21st Century*, Vol. 23. Urban Affairs Annual Reviews: Sage Publications.

Blauner, R. (1964) *Alienation and Freedom*, Chicago: Chicago University Press.

Block, F. (1994) 'The Roles of the State in the Economy' in Smelser, N. and Swedberg, R. (eds) *The Handbook of Economic Sociology*, Princeton NJ: Princeton University Press.

Boer, L. (1990) '(In)formalization: the Forces Beyond', *International Journal of Urban and Regional Research*, Vol. 14. No. 3. pp. 404–22.

Boris, E. (1988) 'Homework and Women's Rights: the Case of the Vermont Knitters' in Boris, E. and Daniels, C. (eds) *Homework: Historical and Contemporary Perspectives on Paid Labour at Home*, Urbana: University of Illinois Press.

Bradshaw, A. and Holmes, H. (1989) *Living on the Edge*, Tyneside: Tyneside Child Poverty Action Group.

Bresnen, M. (1985) 'The Flexibility of Recruitment in the Construction Industry: Formalization or Re-Casualization', *Sociology*, Vol. 9. pp. 108–24.

Bromley, R. and Gerry, C. (eds) (1979) *Casual Work and Poverty in Third World Cities*, Chichester: John Wiley.

Bryson, A. and Jacobs, J. (1992) *Policing the Workshy*, Aldershot: Avebury.

Buechler, J.M. (1987) 'A Review – Guest, Intruder, Settler, Ethnic Minority or Citizen: the Sense and Nonsense of Borders' in Buechler, H.C. and Buechler, J.M. (eds) *Migrants in Europe: the Role of Family, Labor and Politics*, Westport, Connecticut: Greenwood Press.

Bulletin on Women and Employment in the EC (1994) No. 4. April, Manchester: UMIST.

Bulmer, M. (1986) *Neighbours: the Work of Philip Abrams*, Cambridge: Cambridge University Press.

Burns, S. (1977) *The Household Economy*, Boston: Beacon Press.

Callaghan, B. (1986) 'Flexibility: a UK Trade Union Response', *Social and Labour Bulletin*, No. 2. Geneva: ILO.

Callaghan, P. and Hartmann, H. (1991) *Contingent Work: a Chart Book on Part-time and Temporary Employment*, Washington DC: Economic Policy Institute.

Castells, M. and Portes, A. (1989) 'World Underneath: the Origins, Dynamics and Effects of the Informal Economy' in Portes, A., Castells, M. and Benton, L.A. (eds) *The Informal Economy: Studies in Advanced and Less Developed Countries*, Baltimore: John Hopkins University Press.

CDEM, Bureau of the Steering Committee for Employment and Labour, (1995) *Children and Work in Europe: Report of the Study Group on Children's Work*, Strasbourg: Council of Europe.

Chadeau, A. (1985) 'Measuring Household Activities: Some International Comparisons', *The Review of Income and Wealth*, Vol. 31. No. 3. pp. 237–53.

Chamot, D. (1988) 'Blue-Collar, White-Collar: Homeworker Problems' in Christensen, K.E. (ed.) *The New Era of Homebased Work*, Boulder: Westview Press.

Chavez, L.R. (1992) 'Paradise at a Cost: The Incorporation of Undocumented Mexican Immigrants into a Local Level Labour Market' in Bustamante, J.A., Reynolds, C.W. and Hinojosa Ojeda, R.A. (eds) *US-Mexico Relations: Labour Market Interdependence*, Stanford, California: Stanford University Press.

Chinoy, E. (1955) *Automobile Workers and the American Dream*, New York: Doubleday Publications.

Christensen, K. (1988) 'Home-based Clerical Work: No Simple Truth, No Single Reality' in Boris, E. and Daniels, C.R. (eds) *Homework: Historical and Contemporary Perspectives on Paid Labor at Home*, Urbana: University of Illinois Press.

Christie, I. (1994) 'Flexibility and Its Discontents: New Perspectives on the Future of Work', *Policy Studies*, Vol. 15. No. 4. pp. 22–33.

Chronaki, Z., Hadjimichalis, C., Labrianidis, L. and Vaiou, D. (1993) 'Diffused Industrialization in Thessaloniki: from Expansion to Crisis', *International Journal of Urban and Regional Research*, Vol. 17. No. 2. pp. 178–94.

Collinson, S. (1993) *Europe and International Migration*, London: Royal Institute of International Affairs.

Commission of the European Communities (1991) *Employment in Europe*, Luxembourg: Office for Official Publications of the European Communities.

Contini, B. (1982) 'The Second Economy of Italy' in Tanzi, V. (ed.) *The Underground Economy in the United States and Abroad*, Mass: Lexington Books.

Contini, B. (1989) 'The Irregular Economy of Italy: a Survey of Contributions' in Feige, E.L. (ed.) *The Unofficial Economies*, Cambridge: Cambridge University Press.

Cook, D. (1989) *Rich Law, Poor Law: Different Responses to Tax and Supplementary Benefit Fraud*, Milton Keynes: Open University Press.

Cornelius, W.A. (1992) 'From Sojourners to Settlers: The Changing Profile of Mexican Immigration to the United States', in Bustamante, J.A., Reynolds, C.W. and Hinojosa Ojeda, R.A. (eds) *US-Mexico Relations: Labour Market Interdependence*, Stanford, California: Stanford University Press.

Cornuel, D. and Duriez, B. (1985) 'Local Exchange and State Intervention' in Redclift, N. and Mingione, E. (eds) *Beyond Employment*, Oxford: Blackwell.

Costello, C.B. (1988) 'Clerical Home-Based Work: a Case Study of Work and Family, in Christensen, K.E. (ed.) *The New Era of Home-Based Work*, Bouldner: Westview Press.

Cousins, C. (1994) 'A Comparison of the Labour Market Position of Women in Spain and the UK with Reference to the Flexible Labour Debate', *Work, Employment and Society*, Vol. 8. No. 1. pp. 45–67.

Crow, G. (1989) 'The Use of the Concept "Strategy" in Recent Sociological Literature', *Sociology*, Vol. 23. No. 1. pp. 1–24.

Cummings, S. (ed.) (1980) *Self-Help in Urban America: Patterns of Minority Business Enterprise*, New York: Kennikat Press.

Dallalfar, A. (1994) 'Iranian Women as Immigrant Entrepreneurs', *Gender and Society*, Vol. 8. No. 4. pp. 541–61.

Damianos, D., Demoussis, M. and Kasimis, C. (1992) 'The Empirical Dimension of Multiple Job-Holding Agriculture in Greece', *Sociologia Ruralis*, Vol. 31–2. pp. 37–47.

D'Amico, R. (1984) 'Does Employment During High School Impair Academic Progress?' *Sociology of Education*, Vol. 57. pp. 152–64.

Dangler, J.F. (1986) 'Industrial Homework in the Modern World Economy' *Contemporary Crises*, Vol. 10. pp. 257–79.

Dangler, J.F. (1994) *Hidden in the Home: the Role of Waged Homework in the Modern World Economy*, Albany: State University of New York Press.

Davies, J. (1985) 'Rules not Laws: Outline of an Ethnographic Approach to Economics' in Roberts, B., Finnegan, R., Gallie, D. (eds) *New Approaches to Economic Life: Economic Restructuring, Unemployment and the Social Division of Labour*, Manchester: Manchester University Press.

Davies, C. and Rosser, J. (1987) 'Women's Career Paths: a Male Pathway Unwilling to Bend', *The Health Service Journal*, February.

DeGrazia, R. (1984) *Clandestine Employment*, Geneva: International Labour Office.

De Soto, H. (1989) *The Other Path*, New York: Harper and Row.

Dex, S. and Walters, P. (1989) 'Women's Occupational Status in Britain, France and the USA: Explaining the Difference', *Industrial Relations Journal*, No. 3. pp. 203–12.

Ditton, J. and Brown, R. (1981) 'Why Don't They Revolt: Invisible Income as a Neglected Dimension of Runciman's Relative Deprivation Thesis', *British Journal of Sociology*, Vol. 32. pp. 521–30.

duRivage, V. and Jacobs, D. (1989) 'Home-Based Work: Labour's Choices' in Boris, E. and Daniels, C. (eds) *Homework: Historical and Contemporary Perpsectives on Paid Labour at Home*, Chicago: University of Illinois Press.

Edgell, S. and Hart, G. (1988) *Informal Work: a Case Study of Moonlighting Firemen*, Salford: Salford Papers in Sociology and Anthropology.

Edin, K. (1991) 'Surviving the Welfare System: How AFDC Recipients Make Ends Meet in Chicago' *Social Problems*, Vol. 38. No. 4. pp. 462–74.

Eping-Andersen, G. (1994) 'Welfare States and the Economy' in Smelser, N. and Swedberg, R. (eds) *The Handbook of Economic Sociology*, Princeton: Princeton University Press.

Eyler, D.R. (1989) *The Executive Moonlighter: Building Your Next Career without Leaving Your Present Job*, New York: John Wiley and Sons.

Fagan, C. and Rubery, J. (1996) 'The Salience of the Part-Time Divide in the European Union', *European Sociological Review*, Vol. 12. No. 3. pp. 227–50.

Feagin, J. and Smith, M.P. (1987) 'Cities and the New International Division of Labour: an Overview' in Feagin, J. and Smith, M.P. (eds) *The Capitalist City*, New York: Blackwell.

Feige, E.L. (1977) 'The Anatomy of the Underground Economy' in Alessandrini, S. and Dallago, B. (eds) *The Unofficial Economy*, Aldershot: Gower.

Feige, E.L. (1979) 'How Big is the Irregular Economy?', *Challenge*, Nov–Dec. pp. 5–13.

Feige, E.L. (1980) 'A New Perspective on Macroeconomic Phenomena. The Theory and Measurement of the Unobserved Sector of the United States: Causes, Consequences and Implications' *Mimeographed*. Wassenaar: Netherlands Institute for Advanced Study.

Feige, E.L. (1989) 'The Meaning and Measurement of the Underground Economy' in Feige, E.L. (ed.) *The Underground Economies*, Cambridge: Cambridge University Press.

Felstead, A. and Jewson, N. (1996) *Homeworkers in Britain*, London: HMSO.

Ferman, L. and Berndt, L. (1981) 'The Irregular Economy' in Henry, S. (ed.) *Can I Have It In Cash*, London: Astragal Books.

Fernandez-Kelly, M.P. and Garcia, A.M. (1989a) 'Informalization at the Core: Hispanic Women, Homework and the Advanced Capitalist State' in Portes, A., Castello, M. and Benton, L. *The Informal Economy: Studies in Advanced and Less Developed Countries*, Baltimore: John Hopkins University Press.

Fernandez-Kelly, M.P. and Garcia, A.M. (1989b) 'Hispanic Women and Homework: Women in the Informal Economy of Miami and Los Angeles', in Boris, E. and Daniels, C. *Homework: Historical and Contemporary Perspectives on Paid Labour at Home*, Chicago: University of Illinois Press.

Finch, J. (1993) 'The Concept of Caring: Feminist and Other Perspectives' in Twigg, J. (ed.) *Informal Care in Europe*, University of York: Social Policy Research Unit.

Finn, D. (1996) *Making Benefits Work: Employment Programmes and Job Creation Measures*, Manchester: Centre for Local Economic Strategies.

Fletcher, R. (1997) 'Evaluating Special Measures for the Unemployed: Some Reflections on Recent UK Experience' *Policy and Politics*, Vol. 25. No. 3. pp. 173–84.

Frey, B.S. and Pommerehne, W.W. (1982) 'Measuring the Hidden Economy: Though This Be Madness, There is Method in It' in Tanzi, V. (ed.) *The Underground Economy in the United States and Abroad*, Mass: Lexington Books.

Friedmann, J.E.T. (1955) *Industrial Society*, New York: Free Press.

Friedman, Kasaba K. (1992) 'New York City: the Underside of the World's Capital' in Smith, J. and Wallerstein, I. (eds) *Creating and Transforming Households: The Constraints of the World Economy*, Paris: Cambridge University Press.

Frobel, H., Heinrichs, J. and Kreye, O. (1980) *The New International Division of Labour*, Cambridge: Cambridge University Press.

Gaffikin, F. and Warf, B. (1993) 'Urban Policy and the Post-Keynesian State in the United Kingdom and the United States', *International Journal of Urban and Regional Research*, Vol. 17. No. 1. pp. 67–84.

Garraty, J.A. (1978) *Unemployment in History: Economic Thought and Public Policy*, New York: Harper and Row.

Gershuny, J. and Miles, I.D. (1985) 'Towards a New Social Economics' in Roberts, B., Finnegan, R. and Gallie, D. (eds) *New Approaches to Economic Life: Economic Restructuring, Unemployment and the Social Division of Labour*, Manchester: Manchester University Press.

Gershuny, J. and Pahl, R.E. (1981) 'Work outside Employment: Some Preliminary Speculations' in Henry, S. (ed.) *Can I Have it in Cash*, London: Astragal Books.

Gershuny, J. (1978) *After Industrial Society*, London: Macmillan.

Gershuny, J. (1983) *Social Innovation and the Division of Labour*, Oxford: Oxford University Press.

Gershuny, J. (1988) 'Time, Technology and the Informal Economy' in R.E. Pahl, (ed.) *On Work: Historical, Comparative and Theoretical Approaches*, Oxford: Blackwell.

Glatzner, W. and Berger, R. (1988) 'Household Composition, Social Networks and Household Production in Germany' in Pahl, R.E. (ed.) *On Work: Historical, Comparative and Theoretical Approaches*, Oxford: Blackwell.

Godard, F. (1985) 'How Do Ways of Life Change?' in Redclift, N. and Mingione, E. (eds) *Beyond Employment: Household, Gender and Subsistence*, Oxford: Blackwell.

Goldthorpe, J.H., Lockwood, D., Bechhofer, F. and Platt, J. (1968) *The Affluent Worker: Industrial Attitudes and Behaviour*, London: Cambridge University Press.

Gouldner, A.W. (1960) 'The Norm of Reciprocity: A Preliminary Statement' *American Sociological Review*, Vol. 25. No. 2. pp. 161–82.

Green, D.L. (1990) 'High School Student Employment in Social Context: Adolescent's Perceptions of the Role of Part-Time Work', *Adolescence*, Vol. 25. pp. 425–34.

Greenberger, E. and Steinberg, L.D. (1986) *When Teenagers Work: the Psychological and Social Costs of Adolescent Employment*, New York: Basil Books.

Grieco, M. (1987) 'Family Networks and the Closure of Employment' in Lee, G. and Loveridge, R. (eds) *The Manufacture of Disadvantage*, Milton Keynes: Open University Press.

Grint, K. (1991) *The Sociology of Work: an Introduction*, Cambridge: Polity Press.

Gutman, H.G. (1988) 'Work, Culture and Society in Industrializing America, 1815–1919' in Pahl, R.E. (ed.) *On Work: Historical, Comparative and Theoretical Approaches*, Oxford: Blackwell.

Gutmann, P.M. (1977) 'The Subterranean Economy' *Financial Analysts Journal*, No. 33. pp. 24–7.

Gutmann, P.M. (1979) 'Statistical Illusions, Mistaken Policies' *Challenge*, Nov–Dec. pp. 14–17.

Hadjicostandi, J. (1990) 'Facon: Women's Formal and Informal Work in the Garment Industry in Kavala, Greece' in Ward, K. (eds) *Women*

Workers and Global Restructuring, New York: ILR Press.

Hadjimichalis, C. and Vaiou, D. (1988) 'Capital Restructuring and Flexible Labour Markets in Northern Greece' in Hadjimichalis, C. and Komninos, N. (eds) *Changing Labour Processes and New Forms of Urbanization*, Thessaloniki: Transactions of the Samos International Seminar.

Hadjimichalis, C. and Vaiou, D. (1990) 'Flexible Labour Markets and Regional Development in Northern Greece', *International Journal of Urban and Regional Research*, Vol. 14. No. 3 pp. 1–24.

Hakim, C. (1989) 'Workforce Restructuring, Social Insurance Coverage and the Black Economy', *Journal of Social Policy*, Vol. 18. No. 3. pp. 471–503.

Hakim, C. (1992) 'Unemployment, Marginal Work and the Black Economy' in McLaughlin, E. (ed.) *Understanding Employment: New Perspectives on Active Labour Market Policies*, London: Routledge.

Hamilton, G.G. (1994) 'Civilizations and the Organization of Economies' in Smelser, N. and Swedberg, R. (eds) *The Handbook of Economic Sociology*, Princeton: Princeton University Press.

Handy, C. (1984) *The Future of Work: a Guide to a Changing Society*, Oxford: Blackwell.

Harding, P. and Jenkins, R. (1989) *The Myth of the Hidden Economy*, Milton Keynes: Open University Press.

Hareven, T.K. (1982) *Family Time and Industrial Time*, New York: Cambridge University Press.

Hareven, T.K. (1990) 'A Complex Relationship: Family Strategies and the Processes of Economic and Social Change' in Friedland, R. and Robertson, A.F. (eds) *Beyond the Marketplace: Rethinking Economy and Society*, New York: Aldine de Gruyter.

Harris, C.C. (1987) *Redundancy and Recession in South Wales*, Oxford: Blackwell.

Hart, K. (1973) 'Informal Economic Opportunities and Urban Employment in Ghana', *Journal of Modern African Studies*, Vol. 11, pp. 61–89.

Hartmann, H. (1981) 'The Family as the Locus of Gender, Class and Political Struggle: the Example of Housework', *Signs*, Vol. 6. No. 3, pp. 366–94.

Harvey, D. (1989) *The Condition of Postmodernity*, Oxford: Blackwell.

Henry, S. (1981) *Can I Have It In Cash*, London: Astragal Books.

Henry, S. (1982) 'The Working Unemployed', *Sociological Review*, No. 30.

Henry, S. and Mars, G. (1978) 'Crime at Work: the Social Construction of Amateur Property Theft', *Sociology*, Vol. 12. pp. 245–63.

Hirst, P.Q. and Zeitlin, J. (eds.) (1989) *Reversing Industrial Decline*, Leamington Spa Berg.

Hobsbawm, E.J. (1964) *Labouring Men*, London: Weidenfeld and Nicolson.

Hoel, B. (1982) 'Contemporary Clothing Sweatshops', in West, J. (ed.) *Women, Work and the Labour Market*, London: Routledge and Kegan Paul.

Holmes, J. (1986) 'The Organization and Locational Structure of Production in Subcontracting' in Scott, A. and Storper, M. (eds.) *Production, Work, Territory*, Boston: Allen and Unwin.

Howe, L. (1990) *Being Unemployed in Northern Ireland*, Cambridge: Cambridge University Press.

Hoyman, M. (1987) 'Female Participation in the Informal Economy: a Neglected Issue' in Ferman, L., Henry, S. and Hoyman, M. (eds) *The Annals of the American Academy of Political and Social Science: the Informal Economy*, Newbury Park, Beverly Hills: Sage Publications.

Hudson, R. (1986) 'Producing an Industrial Wasteland: Capital, Labour and the State in North East England' in R. Martin and B. Rowthorn, (eds) *The Geography of Deindustrialization*, London, Macmillan.

Ironmoner, D. (ed.) (1989) *Households Work: Productive Activities, Women and Income in the Household Economy*, Australia: Allen and Unwin.

Jackson, R. (1995) *What Can Active Labour Market Policy Do?* New York: Centre for Economic Performance, Discussion Paper No. 226.

Jamal, M. (1986) 'Moonlighting: Personal, Social and Organizational Consequences', *Human Relations*, Vol. 39. No. 11. pp. 977–90.

Jessop, B. (1991) 'Thatcherism and Flexibility: The White Heat of a Post-Fordist Revolution' in Jessop, B., Kastendiek, H., Nielsen, K. and Pederson, O.K. (eds) *The Politics of Flexibility: Restructuring State and Industry in Britain, Germany and Scandinavia*, Aldershot: Edward Elgar.

Jordan, B. (1992) *Trapped in Poverty?*, London: Routledge.

Kofman, E. and Sales, R. (1992) 'Towards Fortress Europe?' *Women's Studies International Forum*, Vol. 15. No.1. pp. 29–39.

Langfeldt, E. (1989) 'The Underground Economy in the Federal Republic of Germany: a Preliminary Assessment' in Feige, E.L. (ed.) *The Unofficial Economies*, Cambridge: Cambridge University Press.

Lash, S. (1994) 'The Making of an Underclass: neo-liberalism versus corporatism' in P. Brown and R. Crompton (eds) *A New Europe? Economic Restructuring and Social Exclusion*, London: UCL Press.

Lavalette, M., Hobbs, S., Lindsay, S. and McKechnie, J. (1995) 'Child Employment in Britain: Policy, Myth and Reality', *Youth and Policy*, No. 47.

Laws, G. (1989) 'Privatization and Dependency on the Local Welfare State' in Wolch, J. and Dear, M. (eds) *The Power of Geography: How Territory Shapes Social Life*, Boston: Unwin Hyman.

Lazaridis, G. (1996) 'Immigration to Greece: A Critical Evaluation of Greek Policy', *New Community*, Vol. 22. No. 2. pp. 335–48.

Lee, R.M. (1993) *Doing Research on Sensitive Topics*, London: Sage Publications.

Leira, A. (1993) 'Concepts of Care: Loving, Thinking and Doing' in Twigg, J. (ed.) *Informal Care in Europe*, University of York: Social Policy Research Unit.

Leitner, H. (1990) 'Cities in Pursuit of Economic Growth: the local state as Entrepreneur', *Political Geography Quarterly*, Vol. 9. pp. 146–70.

Leman, J. (1997) 'Undocumented Migrants in Brussels: Diversity and the Anthropology of Illegality', *New Community*, Vol. 23. No. 1.

Lenz, E. and Myerhoff, B. (1985) *The Feminization of America*, Los Angeles, J.P. Tarcher.

Leonard, M. (1992) 'The Modern Cinderellas: Women and the Contract Cleaning Industry in Belfast' in Arber, S. and Gilbert, N. (eds) *Women and Working Lives: Divisions and Change*, London: Macmillan.

Leonard, M. (1994) *Informal Economy in Belfast*, Aldershot: Avebury.

Leonard, M. (1997) 'Women Caring and Sharing in Belfast' in Byrne, A. and Leonard, M. (eds) *Women and Irish Society: a Sociological Reader*, Belfast: Beyond the Pale Publications.

Leonard, M. (forthcoming) 'Child Work in the UK 1970–1997' in Lavalette, M. (ed.) *Child Labour in a Developed Society*, Liverpool: Liverpool University Press.

Lever, A. (1988) 'Capital, Gender and Skill: Women Homeworkers in Rural Spain', *Feminist Review*, No. 30. pp. 4–24.

Light, H.K., Hertsgaard, D. and Martin, R.E. (1985) 'Farm Children's Work in the Family', *Adolescence*, Vol. 20.

Lim, L.Y.C. (1983) 'Capitalism, Imperialism and Patriarchy: the Dilemma of Third-World Women Workers in Multinational Factories' in Nash, J. and Fernandez-Kelly, M.P. (eds) *Women, Men and the International Division of Labour*, Albany, New York: State University of New York Press.

Lipietz, A. (1988) *Mirages and Miracles: the Crisis of Global Fordism*, London: Verso.

Lobo, F.M. (1990a) 'Irregular Work in Spain' in Barthelemy, P., Miguelez, F., Mingione, E., Pahl, R. and Wenig, A. *Underground Economy and Irregular Forms of Employment, Final Synthesis Report*, Luxembourg: Commission of the European Communities.

Lobo, F.M. (1990b) 'Irregular Work in Portugal' in Barthelemy, P., Miguelez, F., Mingione, E., Pahl, R. and Wenig, A. *Underground Economy and Irregular Forms of Employment, Final Synthesis Report*, Luxembourg: Commission of the European Communities.

Lobo, F.M. (1990c) 'The Role of the Market in Irregular Work' in Barthelemy, P., Miguelez, F., Mingione, E., Pahl, R. and Wenig, A. *Underground Economy and Irregular Forms of Employment, Final Synthesis Report*, Luxembourg: Commission of the European Communities.

Lowenthal, M. (1981) 'Non-Market Transactions in an Urban Community' in Henry, S. (ed.) *Can I Have It In Cash?*, London: Astragal Books.

Lozano, B. (1989) *The Invisible Workforce: Transforming American Business with Outside and Homebased Workers*, New York: Free Press.

MacDonald, R. (1994) 'Fiddly Jobs, Undeclared Working and the Something for Nothing Society', *Work, Employment and Society*, Vol. 8. No. 4. pp. 507–30.

McGuire, R.H. and Woodsong, C. (1992) 'Binghamton: the Secrets of a Backwater' in Smith, J. and Wallerstein, I. (eds) *Creating and Transforming Households: the Constraints of the World Economy*, Paris: Cambridge University Press.

McKechnie, J., Lindsay, S. and Hobbs, S. (1996) 'Child Employment: A Neglected Topic?' *The Psychologist*, pp. 219–22.

Malcolmson, R.W. (1988) 'Ways of Getting a Living in Eighteenth Century England' in Pahl, R. (ed.) *On Work: Historical, Comparative and Theoretical Approaches*, Oxford: Blackwell.

Malinowski, B. (1984) 'The Primitive Economics of the Trobriand Islanders' in Littler, C.R. (ed.) *The Experience of Work*, London: Heinemann.

Mattera, P. (1985) *Off the Books: the Rise of the Underground Economy*, New York: St Martin's Press.

Menjivar, C. (1997) 'Immigrant Kinship Networks and the Impact of the

Receiving Context: Salvadorans in San Francisco in the early 1990s', *Social Problems*, Vol. 44. No. 1. pp. 104–23.

Meulders, D. and Plasman, R. (1990) *Women in Atypical Employment*, V/1426/89-FR, Brussels: Commission of the European Communities.

Mies, M. (1986) *Patriarchy and Accumulation on a World Scale*, Atlantic Highlands, NJ: Zed Books Ltd.

Miles, R. (1990) 'Whatever Happened to the Sociology of Migration?, *Work, Employment and Society*, Vol. 4. No. 2. pp. 281–98.

Milkman, R. and Townsley, E. (1994) 'Gender and the Economy' in Smelser, N. and Swedberg, R. (eds) *The Handbook of Economic Sociology*, Princeton: Princeton University Press.

Minford, P. (1983) *Unemployment: Cause and Cure*, Oxford: Martin Robertson.

Mingione, E. (1987) 'Urban Survival Strategies, Family Structure and Informal Practices' in Smith, M.P. and Feagin, J.R. (eds.) *The Capitalist City: Global Restructuring and Community Politics*, Oxford: Basil Blackwell.

Mingione, E. (1988) 'Work and Informal Activities in Southern Urban Italy' in Pahl, R.E. (ed.) *On Work: Historical, Comparative and Theoretical Approaches*, Oxford: Blackwell.

Mingione, E. (1990a) 'Old and New Areas of "Travail au Noir"' in Barthelemy, P., Miguelez, F., Mingione, E., Pahl, R. and Wenig, A. *Underground Economy and Irregular Forms of Employment, Final Synthesis Report*, Luxembourg: Commission of the European Communities.

Mingione, E. (1990b) 'The Case of Italy' in Barthelemy, P., Migueliz, F., Mingione, E., Pahl, R. and Wenig, A. *Underground Economy and Irregular Forms of Employment, Final Synthesis Report*, Luxembourg: Commission of the European Communities.

Mingione, E. (1990c) 'The Case of Greece' in Barthelemy, P., Migueliz, F., Mingione, E., Pahl, R. and Wenig, A. *Underground Economy and Irregular Forms of Employment, Final Synthesis Report*, Luxembourg: Commission of the European Communities.

Mingione, E. (1991) *Fragmented Societies. a Sociology of Economic Life Beyond the Market Paradigm*, Oxford: Blackwell.

Mingione, E. (1994a) *The Informal Sector: Follow-up to the White Paper*, Report to the European Commission's Employment Task Force (Directorate General V), Luxembourg: Commission of the European Communities.

Mingione, E. (1994b) 'Life Strategies and Social Economics in the Postfordist Age', *International Journal of Urban and Regional Research*, Vol. 18. No. 1. pp. 24–45.

Mitter, S. (1986) 'Industrial Restructuring and Manufacturing Homework: Immigrant Women in the UK Clothing Industry', *Capital and Class*, Vol. 27. pp. 37–80.

Molefsky, B. (1982) 'America's Underground Economy' in Tanzi, V. (ed.) *The Underground Economy in the United States and Abroad*, Mass: Lexington Books.

Morokvasic, M. (1987) 'Immigrants in the Parisian Garment Industry', *Work, Employment and Society*, Vol. 1. No. 4. pp. 441–42.

Morris, L.D. (1984) 'Patterns of Social Activity and Post-Redundancy Labour

Market Experience' *Sociology*, Vol. 18. pp. 339–352.

Morris, L.D. (1985) 'Local Social Networks and Domestic Organisation' *Sociological Review*. Vol. 33. pp. 327–42.

Morris, L.D. (1987) 'Local Social Polarization: a Case Study of Hartlepool', *International Journal of Urban and Regional Research*, Vol. 11. pp. 331–50.

Morris, L.D. (1994) 'Informal Aspects of Social Divisions' *International Journal of Urban and Regional Research*, Vol. 18. No. 1. pp. 112–26.

Morris, L. and Irwin, S. (1992) 'Unemployment and Informal Support: Dependency, Exclusion or Participation?' *Work, Employment and Society*, Vol. 6. No. 2. pp. 185–207.

Munz, R. (1996) 'A Continent of Migration: European Mass Migration in the Twentieth Century', *New Community*, Vol. 22. No. 2. pp. 201–26.

Murphy, M. (1982) 'Comparative Estimates of the Value of Household Work in the United States for 1976', *Review of Income and Wealth*, Vol. 28. pp. 29–43.

Murray, F. (1988a) 'The Decentralisation of Production – the Decline of the Mass-Collective Worker' in Pahl, R. (ed.) *On Work: Historical, Comparative and Theoretical Approaches*, Oxford: Blackwell.

Murray, R. (1988b) 'Life after Henry (Ford)' *Marxism Today*, October.

Myles, J. (1990) 'States, Labor Markets and Life Cycles' in Friedland, R. and Robertson, A.F. (eds) *Beyond the Marketplace: Rethinking Economy and Society*, New York: Aldine de Gruyter.

Neef, R. (1992) 'The New Poverty and Local Government Social Policies: a West German Perspective', *International Journal of Urban and Regional Research*, Vol. 16. No. 2. pp. 202–21.

Nelson, M. (1988) 'Providing Family Day Care: an Analysis of Home-Based Work', *Social Problems*, Vol. 35. No. 1. pp. 78–94.

Nielsen, L. (1991) 'Flexibility, Gender and Local Labour Markets – Some Examples from Denmark', *International Journal of Urban and Regional Research*, Vol. 15. No.1. pp. 42–53.

Offe, C. and Heinz, R.G. (1996) 'Beyond the Labour Market: Reflections on a New Definition of "Domestic" Welfare Production', in Offe, C., *Modernity and the State*, Cambridge: Polity Press.

Offe, C. and Heinze, R.G. (1992) *Beyond Employment: Time, Work and the Informal Economy*, Cambridge: Polity Press.

O'Higgins, M. (1980) 'Measuring the Hidden Economy: a Review of Evidence and Methodologies' *Mimeographed*. London: Outer Policy Circle.

O'Higgins, M. (1989) 'Assessing the Underground Economy in the United Kingdom' in Feige, E.L. (ed.) *The Underground Economies*, Cambridge: Cambridge University Press.

Organization for Economic Cooperation and Development (OECD) (1986) 'Concealed Employment' in *Employment Outlook 1986*, Paris: OECD.

Organization for Economic Cooperation and Development (OECD) (1980) 'Measuring the Volume of Unrecorded Employment' *Mimeographed*. MAS/WP 7(80)3 Paris: OECD.

Organization for Economic Cooperation and Development (OECD) (1978) 'Methods Used to Estimate the Extent of Tax Evasion' *Mimeographed*. MAS/WP 7(78)1. Paris: OECD.

Ormerod, P. (1994) 'Why Western Employment Policy is Going Around in Circles', *Demos Quarterly: Special Issue, The End of Unemployment: Bringing Work to Life*, No. 2.

Pahl, R.E. (1980) 'Employment, Work and the Domestic Division of Labour', *International Journal of Urban and Regional Research*, Vol. 4. No. 1. pp. 1–20.

Pahl, R.E. (1984) *Divisions of Labour*, Oxford: Blackwell.

Pahl, R.E. (1988) *On Work: Historical, Comparative and Theoretical Approaches*, Oxford: Blackwell.

Pahl, R.E. (1990) 'The Black Economy in the United Kingdom' in Barthelemy, P., Miguelez, F., Mingione, E., Pahl, R. and Wenig, A. *Underground Economy and Irregular Forms of Employment, Final Synthesis Report*, Luxembourg: Commission of the European Communities.

Pahl, R.E. and Wallace, C. (1985) 'Household Work Strategies in Economic Recession' in Redclift, N. and Mingione, E. (eds) *Beyond Employment*, Oxford: Blackwell.

Peattie, L.R. (1980) 'Anthropological Perspectives on the Concepts of Dualism, the Informal Sector and Marginality in Developing Urban Economies', *International Regional Science*, Vol. 5. pp. 1–31.

Pedersen, P.O., Sverrisson, A. and Van Dijk, M.P. (eds) (1994) *Flexible Specialization*, London: Intermediate Technology Publications.

Phizacklea, A. (1987) 'Minority Women and Economic Restructuring: the Case of Britain and the Federal Republic of Germany', *Work, Employment and Society*, Vol. 1. No. 3. pp. 309–25.

Phizacklea, A. (1990) *Unpacking the Fashion Industry: Gender, Racism and Class in Production*, London: Routledge.

Pinnaro, G. and Pugliese, E. (1985) 'Informalization and Social Resistance: the case of Naples' in Redclift, N. and Mingione, E. (eds) *Beyond Employment: Household, Gender and Subsistence*, Oxford: Blackwell.

Piore, M. and Sabel, C. (1984) *The Second Industrial Divide: Possibilities for Prosperity*, New York: Basic Books.

Pleck, J. (1995) *Working Wives, Working Husbands*, Beverly Hills, CA: Sage Publications.

Polanyi, K. (1957) *The Great Transformation*, Boston: Beacon Press.

Pollert, A. (1988) 'Dismantling Flexibility', *Capital and Class*, No. 34. pp. 42–75.

Portes, A. (1981) 'Unequal Exchange and the Urban Informal Sector' in Portes, A. and Walton, J. (eds) *Labour, Class and the International System*, New York: Academic Press.

Portes, A. (1995) 'Economic Sociology and the Sociology of Immigration: A Conceptual Overview' in Portes, A. (ed.) *The Economic Sociology of Immigration: Essays on Networks, Ethnicity and Entrepreneurship*, New York: Russell Sage Foundation.

Portes, A. and Sassen-Koob, S. (1987) 'Making it Underground: Comparative Material on the Urban Informal Sector in Western Market Economies', *American Journal of Sociology*, Vol. 93. pp. 30–61.

Portes, A. and Schauffler, R. (1992) *The Informal Economy in Latin America: Definition, Measurement and Policies*, Working Paper No. 5. Baltimore, John Hopkins University.

176   *References*

Redclift, N. and Mingione, E. (eds) (1985) *Beyond Employment: House-hold, Gender and Subsistence*, Oxford: Blackwell.
Repak, T.A. (1994) 'Labour Recruitment and the Lure of the Capital: Central American Migrants in Washington DC', *Gender and Society*, Vol. 8. No. 4. pp. 507–24.
Roberts, B. (1987) 'The Other Working Class: Uncommitted Labor in Britain, Spain and Mexico' in Kohn, M.L. *Cross-National Research in Sociology*, American Sociological Association Presidential Series, Newbury Park: Sage Publications.
Roberts, B. (1989) 'Employment Structure, Life Cycle and Life Chances: Formal and Informal Sectors in Guadalajara' in A. Portes, M. Castells and L.A. Benton, (eds) *The Informal Economy: Studies in Advanced and Less Developed Countries*, Baltimore, John Hopkins University Press.
Roberts, B. (1991) 'Household Coping Strategies and Urban Poverty in a Comparative Perspective', in Gottdiener, M. and Pickvance, C.G. (eds) *Urban Life in Transition*, Vol. 39. Urban Affairs Annual Reviews, pp. 135–68. Newbury Park, California: Sage.
Roberts, B. (1994) 'Informal Economy and Family Strategies' International Journal of Urban and Regional Research, Vol. 18. No. 1. pp. 6–23.
Romaniszyn, K. (1996) 'The Invisible Community: Undocumented Polish Workers in Athens', *New Community*, Vol. 22. No. 2. pp. 321–33.
Ronco, W. and Peattie, L. (1988) 'Making Work: a Perspective from Social Science' in R.E. Pahl, (ed.) *On Work: Historical, Comparative and Theoretical Approaches*, Oxford: Blackwell.
Rose, R. (1985) 'Getting By in the Three Economies: the Resources of Official, Unofficial and Domestic Economies' in Lane, J. (ed.) *State and Market: the Politics of the Public and the Private*, London: Sage Publications.
Rubery, J. (ed.) (1988) *Women and Recession*, London: Routledge and Kegan Paul.
Sahlins, M. (1972) *Stone Age Economics*, Chicago: Aldine Atherton.
Salt, J. (1993) *Migration and Population Change in Europe*, New York: United Nations Institute for Disarmament Research, Working Paper No. 19.
Sassen, S. (1991) 'The Informal Economy' in Mollenkopf, J.H. and Castells, M. (eds.) *Dual City: Restructuring New York*, New York: Russell Sage Foundation.
Sassen, S. (1996) New Employment regimes in Cities: the Impact on Immigrant Workers, *New Community*, Vol. 22. pp. 579–94.
Sassen-Koob, S. (1984) 'The New Labour Demand in World Cities' in Smith, M.P. (ed.) *Cities in Transformation: Capital, Class and Urban Structure*, Beverly Hills, CA: Sage.
Sassen-Koob, S. (1987) 'Growth and Informalization at the Core: a Preliminary Report on New York City' in Smith, M.P. and Feagin, J.R. (eds) *The Capitalist City*, Oxford: Blackwell.
Sassen-Koob, S. (1989) 'New York City's Informal Economy' in Portes, A., Castells, M. and Benton, L. (eds.) *The Informal Economy: Studies in Advanced and Less Developed Countries*, Baltimore: John Hopkins University Press.
Saunders, J.M. and Nee, V. (1996) 'Immigrant Self-Employment: the Family

as Social Capital and the Value of Human Capital', *American Sociological Review*, Vol. 61. pp. 231–49.

Sayer, A. (1989) 'Postfordism in Question', *International Journal of Urban and Regional Research*, Vol. 13. No. 4. pp. 666–95.

Sayers, S. (1988) 'The Need to Work: a Perspective from Philosphy' in Pahl, R.E. (ed.) *On Work: Historical, Comparative and Theoretical Approaches*, Oxford: Blackwell.

Scott, A. (1988) 'Flexible Production Systems and Regional Development: the Rise of New Industrial Spaces in North America and Western Europe', International Journal of Urban and Regional Research, Vol. 12. pp. 171–85.

Shankland, G. (1984) *A Guide to the Informal Economy*: a Work and Society Report, Brighton: Institute of Manpower Studies.

Sheenan, M. and Tomlinson, M. (1996) 'Long-Term Unemployment and the Community Work Programme' in McLaughlin, E. and Quirk, P. (eds) *Policing Aspects of Employment Equality in Northern Ireland*, Belfast: Standing Advisory Committee on Human Rights.

Silver, H. (1989) 'The Demand for Homework: Evidence from the US Census' in Boris, E. and Daniels, C. (eds) on *Homework: Historical and Contemporary Perspectives on Paid Labour at Home*, Chicago: University of Illinois Press.

Silver, H. (1996) 'Only so many Hours in a Day: Time Constraints, Labor Pools and Demand for Consumer Services' *Service Industries Journal*, No. 7. pp. 26–45.

Simcox, D. (1997) 'Immigration and Informalization of the Economy: Enrichment or Atomization of Community', *Population and Environment: A Journal of Interdisciplinary Studies*, Vol. 18. No. 3. pp. 255–81.

Simmons, C. and Kalantaridis, C. (1995) 'Labour Regimes and the Domestic Domain: Manufacturing Garments in Rural Greece', *Work, Employment and Society*, Vol. 9. No. 2. pp. 287–308.

Skolka, J. (1987) 'A Few Facts about the Hidden Economy' in Alessandrini, S. and Dallago, B. (eds.) *The Unofficial Economy: Consequences and Perspectives in Different Economic Systems*, Aldershot: Gower.

Smelser, N.J. (1959) *Social Change in the Industrial Revolution: an Application of Theory to the British Cotton Industry*, Chicago: University of Chicago Press.

Smith, C. (1989) 'Flexible Specialisation, Automation and Mass Production', *Work, Employment and Society*, Vol. 3. No. 2. pp. 203–20.

Smith, J. (1984) 'The Paradox of Women's Employment: the Importance of Being Marginal', *Signs*, Vol. 10. No. 2. pp. 291–310.

Smith, J. (1990) 'All Crises are not the Same: Households in the United States during the Two Crises' in Collins, J. and Gimenez, M. (eds) *Work without Wages: Labour and Self-Employment Within Capitalism*, Albany: State University of New York Press.

Smith, S. (1986) *Britain's Shadow Economy*, Oxford: Clarendon Press.

Smith, J. and Wallerstein, I. (eds.) (1992) *Creating and Transforming Households: the Constraints of the World Economy*, Paris: Cambridge University Press.

Smith, S. and Wied-Nebbeling, S. (1986) *The Shadow Economy in Britain and Germany*, London: Anglo-German Foundation.

Stack, C. (1974) *All Our Kin: Strategies for Survival in a Black Community*, New York: Harper and Row.

Standing, G. (1989) 'The "British Experiment": Structural Adjustment or Accelerated Decline?' in Portes, A., Castells, M. and Benton, L. *The Informal Economy: Studies in Advanced and Less Developed Countries*, Baltimore: John Hopkins University Press.

Standing, G. (1986) 'Meshing Labour Flexibility with Security: an Answer to British Unemployment' *International Labour Review*, No. 125. pp. 87–106.

Stanley, K. and Smith, J. (1992) 'The Detroit Story: the Crucible of Fordism' in Smith, J. and Wallerstein, I. (eds) *Creating and Transforming Households: the Constraints of The World Economy*, Paris: Cambridge University Press.

Steinberg, L., Greenberger, E., Vaux, A. and Rugiero, M. (1981) 'Effects of Early Work Experience on Adolescent Occupational Socialization', *Youth and Society*, Vol. 12. pp. 403–22.

Stepick, A. (1989) 'Miami's Two Informal Sectors' in Portes, A., Castells, M. and Benton, L. (eds) *The Informal Economy: Studies in Advanced and Less Developed Societies*, Baltimore: John Hopkins University Press.

Stepick, A. (1990) 'Community Growth versus Simply Surviving: the Informal Sector of Cubans and Haitians in Miami' in Smith, M.E. (ed.) *Perspectives on the Informal Economy*, Monographs in Economic Anthropology, No. 8. Maryland: United Press of America, Inc.

Stinson, J.F. (1990) 'Multiple Jobholding Up Sharply in the 1980s', *Monthly Labour Review*, No. 113. pp. 3–10.

Susser, I. (1991) 'The Separation of Mothers and Children' in Mollenkopf, J.H. and Castells, M. (eds) *Dual City: Restructuring New York*, New York: Russell Sage Foundations.

Sverrisson, A. (1994) 'Gradual Diffusion of Flexible Techniques in Small and Medium-Size Enterprise Networks' in Pedersen, P.O., Sverisson, A. and van Dijk, M.P. (eds) *Flexible Specialization: The Dynamics of Small-Scale Industries in the South*, London: Intermediate Technology Publications.

Syrett, S. (1993) 'Local Economic Initiatives in Portugal: Reality and Rhetoric', *International Journal of Urban and Regional Research*, Vol. 17. No. 4. pp. 526–46.

Szelenyi, I. (1981) 'Structural Changes and Alternatives to Capitalist Development in the Contemporary Urban and Regional System', *International Journal of Urban and Regional Research*, Vol. 5. No. 1 pp. 1–14.

Tanzi, V. (1982) 'A Second (and More Sceptical Look) at the Underground Economy in the United States' in Tanzi, V. (ed.) *The Underground Economy in the United States and Abroad*, Lexington: Lexington Books Ltd.

Tanzi, V. (1983) 'The Underground Economy in the United States: Annual Estimates 1930–1980', *IMF Staff Papers*, No. 2. pp. 283–305.

Thomas, J.J. (1988) 'The Politics of the Black Economy', *Work, Employment and Society*, Vol. 2. pp. 169–90.

Thomas, J.J. (1990) 'Measuring the Underground Economy: a Suitable

Case for Interdisciplinary Treatment', *American Behavioural Scientist*, Vol. 33. No. 5. pp. 621–37.

Thomas, J.J. (1992) *Informal Economic Activity*, Hemel Hempstead: Harvester Wheatsheaf.

Tilly, C. (1975) *The Formation of Nation States in Western Europe*, Princeton NJ: Princeton University Press.

Tilly, C. (1990) 'Transplanted Networks' in Yans-McLaughlin, V. (ed.) *Immigration Reconsidered*, New York: Oxford University Press.

Tilly, C. and Tilly, C. (1994) 'Capitalist Work and Labor Markets' in Smelser, N. and Swedberg, R. (eds) *The Handbook of Economic Sociology*, Princeton: Princeton University Press.

Tomaney, J. (1990) 'The Reality of Workplace Flexibility' *Capital and Class*, Vol. 40. pp. 29–59.

Tuominen, M. (1994) 'The Hidden Organization of Labour: Gender, Race/Ethnicity and Childcare Work in the Formal and Informal Economy', *Sociological Perspectives*, Vol. 37. No. 2. pp. 229–45.

Twigg, J. (ed.) (1993) *Informal Care in Europe*, University of York: Social Policy Research Unit.

US Department of Labour, Bureau of Labour Statistics (1991) *Working Women: A Chartbook*, Bulletin 2385, Washington, DC: GPO.

van Herpen, A. (1990) *Children and Youngsters in Europe: the New Proletariat?, A Report on Child Labour in Europe*, Luxembourg: Office of the European Commission.

Vanek, J. (1973) *Keeping Busy: Time Spent in Housework*, United States, Ann Arbor: University Microfilms International.

Vinay, P. (1985) 'Family Life Cycle and the Informal Economy in Italy' *International Journal of Urban and Regional Research*, Vol. 9. No. 1. pp. 82–97.

Wainwright, H. (1987) 'The Friendly Mask of Flexibility', *New Statesman*, 17th December.

Waldinger, R. (1992) 'Taking Care of the Guests: the Impact of Immigrants on Services – An Industry Case Study', *International Journal of Urban and Regional Research*, Vol. 16. No. 1. pp. 97–113.

Waldinger, R. and Lapp, M. (1993) 'Back to the Sweatshop or Ahead to the Informal Sector?', *International Journal of Urban and Regional Research*, Vol. 17. No. 1. pp. 6–29.

Warde, A. (1990) 'Household Work Strategies and Forms of Labour: Conceptual and Empirical Issues', *Work, Employment and Society*, Vol. 4. No. 4 pp. 495–515.

Warren, M.R. (1994) 'Exploitation or Cooperation? the Political Basis of Regional Variation in the Italian Informal Economy', *Politics and Society*, Vol. 22. No. 1. pp. 89–115.

Weiss, L. (1987) 'Explaining the Underground Economy: State and Social Structure', *British Journal of Sociology*, Vol. 38. pp. 216–34.

Wenig, A. (1990a) 'The Shadow Economy in the Federal Republic of Germany' in Barthelemy, P., Miguelez, F., Mingione, E., Pahl, R. and Wenig, A. *Underground Economy and Irregular Forms of Employment, Final Synthesis Report*, Luxembourg: Commission of the European Communities.

Wenig, A. (1990b) 'The Impact of the Shadow Economy on the Economic and Social Cohesion and the Role of the State' in Barthelemy, P., Miguelez, F., Mingione, E., Pahl, R. and Wenig, A. *Underground Economy and Irregular Forms of Employment, Final Synthesis Report*, Luxembourg: Commission of the European Communities.

Wheelock, J. (1990) 'Capital Restructuring and the Domestic Economy: Family Self Respect and the Irrelevance of 'Rational Economic Man', *Capital and Class*, Vol. 41. pp. 103–41.

Whipp, R. (1985) 'Labour Market and Communities: a Historical View', *Sociological Review*, Vol. 33. pp. 768–92.

White, B. (1996) 'Globalization and the Child Labour Problem', *Journal of International Development*, Vol. 8. No. 6. pp. 829–40.

Williams S. (1992) *Child Workers in Portugal*, Anti-Slavery International, Child Labour Series No. 12.

Williams, C. and Windebank, J. (1995) 'Black Market Work in the European Community: Peripheral Work for Peripheral Localities?', *International Journal of Urban and Regional Research*, Vol. 19. No. 1. pp. 23–39.

Wilson, D. (1993) 'Everyday Life, Spatiality and Inner City Disinvestment in a US City', *International Journal of Urban and Regional Research*, Vol. 17. No. 4. pp. 578–94.

Windebank, J. (1991) *The Informal Economy in France*, Aldershot: Avebury.

Witte, A. (1987) 'The Nature and Extent of Unrecorded Activity: A Survey Concentrating on Recent US Research' in Alessandrini, S. and Dallago, B. (eds) *The Unofficial Economy*, Aldershot: Gower.

Wolch, J.R. (1989) 'The Shadow State: transformations in the Voluntary Sector' in Wolch, J. and Dear, M. (eds) *The Power of Geography: How Territory Shapes Social Life*, Boston: Unwin Hyman.

Yucel, A.E. (1987) 'Turkish Migrant Workers in the Federal Republic of Germany: A Case Study' in Buechler, H.C. and Buechler, J.M. (eds) *Migrants in Europe: the Role of Family, Labor and Politics*, Westport, Connecticut: Greenwood Press.

Index

181